TURNING TO GOD

Other books by William Barclay

AMBASSADOR FOR CHRIST
AND HE HAD COMPASSION
AND JESUS SAID
GOD'S YOUNG CHURCH
THE KING AND THE KINGDOM
MARCHING ORDERS
THE MEN, THE MEANING, THE MESSAGE OF THE BOOKS
THE OLD LAW AND THE NEW LAW
THE DAILY STUDY BIBLE (17 vols)

Also in this series

THE ALL-SUFFICIENT CHRIST
FLESH AND SPIRIT
COMMUNICATING THE GOSPEL

TURNING TO GOD

A Study of Conversion
in the Book of Acts and Today

by

WILLIAM BARCLAY

THE SAINT ANDREW PRESS
EDINBURGH

First published in 1963 by the Epworth Press

Republished 1978 by
THE SAINT ANDREW PRESS
121 George Street, Edinburgh

© THE SAINT ANDREW PRESS

ISBN 0 7152 0388 6

Printed and bound in Great Britain by
Bell and Bain Ltd., Glasgow

Contents

Quotations from the Bible are normally
made from the *Revised Standard Version*

Foreword

I SHOULD be sadly lacking in courtesy if I did not place on record my very deep appreciation of the honour that has been done to me in the invitation to deliver the A. S. Peake Memorial Lecture.

For me to deliver this lecture is not only an honour and a privilege; it is also an opportunity to try to repay a very great debt of gratitude. My years as a student of Classics and later of Divinity in the University of Glasgow stretched from 1925 until 1932, and to students of my generation A. S. Peake was a most valued guide. I never knew the man, but there can be few students of my generation who did not know his books, and who were not indebted to them. As a commentator, as an apologist for the Christian faith, as a writer of one of the most useful smaller introductions to the New Testament, and, above all, as one who gave us a view of the Bible which satisfied both the mind and the heart, A. S. Peake ranked amongst the greatest of teachers of his day. Great scholar though he was in his own right, he gloried in the title of a theological middle-man; and he mediated to us and to many more the results of the best theological scholarship in an intelligible and a digestible form. Inevitably, much of the work that he did has now to be re-done with the passing of the years, but it is not too much to say that he wrote his name on a generation of students, and pointed to them the path on which their studies must go. He was the possession not of one Church, but of all the Churches.

The subject I have chosen for this lecture is Conversion. It was necessary to limit the biblical material which was to be examined, and so I took the obvious course and limited it to the material in the Book of Acts. It has seemed to me for a long time past that this is a subject which very much needs our thought. Conversion is a word which in our day and generation has been rediscovered, because we have seen again the coming of great evangelical campaigns on both sides of the Atlantic. But it is possible to rediscover a word and yet not fully to rediscover its meaning; and it is even more possible to rediscover what a word once *meant* without discovering what it now must *mean*. Very certainly, conversion is a word which can never be eliminated from the vocabulary of the Christian, but equally certainly the means towards it and the results of it must alter from generation to generation. And, as I have had occasion to say in the lecture, one of the strangest phenomena of the present-day religious situation is that it is rather outside than inside the Church that conversion is expected to happen.

What I have offered is only the merest approach to the subject, but it is my hope and my prayer that it may at least open up again a subject which can never be out of date so long as there are men and women who have not yet called Jesus Christ Lord.

WILLIAM BARCLAY

THE UNIVERSITY OF GLASGOW
June, 1963

If anyone is in Christ, he is a new creation; the old has passed away, behold, the new has come. 2 Corinthians 5^{17}.

Studd lived a bare two years, but it was said at his funeral that he did more in two years than most Christians do in twenty. He withdrew from the Turf, turned the great hall at Tedworth into a meeting-room, wrote to his friends about their souls and laughed when they replied rudely, called on his tailor and his shirt-maker and the man from whom he had bought his cigars, and spoke of Christ. 'All I can say,' said his coachman, 'is that though there's the same skin, there's a new man inside.' J. C. Pollock, *Moody without Sankey*, p. 147.

Chapter I

Conversion in the New Testament

THERE is nothing more significant and revealing than the difference between the pagan and the Christian attitude towards the conflict with sin. Let us begin by looking at this attitude: first, in two pagan writers; second, in one Christian writer; and, finally, in the New Testament itself.

It might be said of Seneca, the Roman Stoic and moralist, that he had a fully developed doctrine of the total depravity of man and of human nature. 'Some sins we have committed,' he writes, 'some we have contemplated, some we have desired, some we have encouraged; in the case of some we are innocent only because we did not succeed' (*On Anger*, 2.28.3). 'We being wicked live among the wicked' (*On Anger*, 3.26.4). He says of the man who on being rebuked promises never to do it again: 'He will go on sinning, and some-one else will sin against him, and the whole of life will be a tossing about amid errors' (*On Anger*, 3.37.3). 'We have all sinned,' he says, 'some in serious, some in trivial things; some from deliberate intention, some by chance impulse, or because we were led away by the wickedness of others; some of us have not stood strongly enough by good resolutions, and have lost our innocence against our will and though still clinging to it; and, not only have we done wrong, but we shall go on doing wrong to the very end of life' (*On Mercy*, 1.3). He talks about how vice does not remain constant, but how in different ages different vices dominate the human scene, at one time adultery, at another a furore for feasting, now concern for the bodily beauty which displays an unbeauteous mind, now ill-controlled liberty, now cruelty, now drunkenness. But however the dominant vice may vary, the verdict we will have to pronounce upon ourselves will be always the same— 'Wicked we are, wicked we have been, and, I regret to add, wicked we always will be' (*On Benefits*, 1.10.2, 3). As Seneca saw life, human nature is wicked, and human nature will never be anything else.

The second witness we will call is Persius, the Roman satirist. Persius speaks of 'filthy Natta, numbed with vice, whose heart is overlaid with brawn, who has no sense of sin, no knowledge of what he is losing, and is sunk so deep that he sends up not even a bubble to the surface'. He prays that God may open the eyes of tyrants that they may 'look on virtue, and pine that they have lost her for ever' (Persius, *Satires*, 3.32-8). A kind of numbing necrosis of sin has fallen upon life, so that a man is even anaesthetized against remorse and regret and repentance, and so that goodness is for ever beyond man's power to attain or even to glimpse.

And now to the other side of the story. John Wesley never underestimated the seriousness of the human situation, but he had something to bring to that human situation which paganism never possessed. He writes: 'I have seen (as far as a thing of this kind can be seen) very many persons changed in a moment from the spirit of fear, horror, despair, to the spirit of love, joy, and peace, and from sinful desire, till then reigning over them, to a pure desire of doing the will of God; him that was a drunkard and is now exemplarily sober; the whoremonger that was, who now abhors the very "garment spotted by the flesh". . . . This is the fact; let any judge of it as they please.' As James Denney said, it is of the very essence of Christianity that it has in it the power to make bad men good. As a reprobate from the submerged criminal class once said after hearing Phillips Brooks preach: 'By God, I believe he could make a good man of me for a week!' Here is the very reverse of the pagan pessimism, the pagan hopelessness, and the pagan despair. Paganism saw nothing for it but to accept the grim fact that man is irremediably and irredeemably evil; Christianity thinks in terms of a dynamic which believes that, as Fosdick puts it in a sermon title, 'No man need stay the way he is'.

Finally, we go to the New Testament itself. There can have been few worse towns anywhere in the world than Corinth. So notorious was Corinth that the verb *korinthiazesthai* had been coined from its name to express drunkenness, immorality, and debauchery. And to that town Christianity came, and as a result of Christianity Paul can write: 'Do you not know that the unrighteous will not inherit the kingdom of God? Do not be deceived; neither the immoral, nor idolaters, nor adulterers, nor homosexuals, nor thieves, nor the greedy, nor drunkards, nor revilers, nor robbers will inherit the kingdom of God. And such were some of you. But you were washed, you were sanctified, you were justified in the name of the Lord Jesus Christ and in the Spirit of our God' (1 Cor 6⁹⁻¹¹). There was in Christianity that changing power which paganism almost completely lacked—and that is precisely what we call conversion.

So, then, let us turn to the New Testament to see what it has to say about conversion; and let us start by examining the word itself. In modern religious language the word *conversion* has acquired a technical sense; it has also acquired certain overtones which connect it, at least in the popular view, with what are termed evangelistic and revivalistic campaigns, with dramatic declarations for Jesus Christ, and sudden and even shattering changes in life. But when we study the evidence of the New Testament we find that the word *conversion* and its allied words have no such technical meaning.

When we turn to the Authorized Version of the New Testament, we may well be surprised to find that the words *convert* and *conversion* occur only eight times between them; and these eight times really reduce themselves to three. Four of the passages (Matt 13¹⁵; Mk 4¹²; Jn 12⁴⁰; Acts 28²⁷) are quotations of Isaiah 6⁹, ¹⁰ in which it is said that the people's heart has become gross and their ears dull, and their eyes have closed, lest they should see or hear or understand, 'and should be *converted*'. Two of the instances come together in James 5¹⁹, ²⁰ where it is said that the man who *converts* a sinner from the error of his ways, not only converts the sinner, but saves a soul from death and hides a multitude of sins. The remaining three instances are in Matthew 18³: 'Except ye be *converted* and become as little children, ye shall not enter into the kingdom of heaven'; Luke 22³², where Jesus says to Peter as He foretells his failure: 'When thou art *converted*, strengthen thy brethren'; Acts 15³, where it is said that Paul and Silas declared 'the *conversion* of the Gentiles'. All these instances are connected with the Greek verbs *epistrephein* and *strephein* and with the allied noun, *epistrophē*.

When we examine other translations of the New Testament, we find that there are seven other instances in which other Greek words have been translated in terms of conversion. These seven instances are connected with three Greek words. (i) Certain translators translate *prosēlutos*, proselyte (Matt 23¹⁵; Acts 2¹⁰, 6⁵, 13⁴³), in some such terms as *a convert to Judaism*. (ii) In Romans 16⁵ and in 1 Corinthians 16¹⁵ certain people are called the *aparchē*, the first-fruits, of Asia and Achaia. Certain translators modernize that into the first *converts* of Asia and Achaia. (iii) In 1 Timothy 3⁶ it is said that the bishop is not to be a *neophutos*, a neophyte, a newly baptized Christian, and again certain translators modernize this into some such phrase as *a recent convert*.

When then we put together the Authorized Version and the bulk of the more modern translations we find that there are fifteen places in the New Testament where the word *conversion* or *convert* may be found. But the highly significant fact is that in not one single instance of them is the word *convert* or *conversion* found in every translation. Let us take four instances and see the amazingly wide variation of translation. In each case for the sake of some standard of comparison we begin by giving the Authorized Version translation.

(i) Matthew 18³:

Verily I say unto you, Except ye be converted, and become as little children, ye shall not enter into the kingdom of heaven.

We now list the various translations:

converted: Authorized Version; Geneva; Rheims.
be turned: Wicliffe.
turn: Tyndale; the Great Bible; the Bishops' Bible; the Revised Version; the Revised Standard Version; Moffatt; Weymouth; C. Kingsley Williams.
turn round: The New English Bible.
turn back: Ferrar Fenton.
turn again: Westminster.
change: Twentieth Century New Testament; E. J. Goodspeed.
change your whole outlook: J. B. Phillips.
unless your hearts are changed: E. V. Rieu.
have a change of heart: The New Testament in Basic English.
become again: Knox.

Here we have no fewer than eleven different translations, although they all centre round the twin ideas of turning and changing.

(ii) Acts 6^5:

Nicolas, a proselyte of Antioch.

proselyte: Authorized Version; Geneva; Revised Version; Revised Standard Version; Moffatt; Weymouth; Knox; Westminster.
comeling: Wicliffe.
convert: Tyndale; the Great Bible; the Bishops' Bible; Ferrar Fenton; E. J. Goodspeed; Twentieth Century New Testament; C. Kingsley Williams; J. B. Phillips.
a former convert to Judaism: New English Bible.
who had become a Jew: The New Testament in Basic English.
stranger: Rheims.

Here we have five different ways of translating the one word.

(iii) 1 Timothy 3⁶:

not a novice (margin, not one newly come to the
   faith).

novice: Authorized Version.

young scholar: Tyndale; the Great Bible; Geneva; the
   Bishops' Bible.

new converted: Wicliffe.

neophyte: Rheims.

a recent convert: Revised Standard Version; Twentieth
   Century New Testament; J. C. W. Wand.

a convert newly baptized: New English Bible.

a new convert: Ferrar Fenton; Moffatt; E. J. Goodspeed;
   Weymouth; C. Kingsley Williams; Knox; A. S. Way;
   Westminster.

not newly taken into the church: The New Testament in Basic
   English.

a beginner in the faith: J. B. Phillips.

Here we have five varied translations and four translations which use the idea of conversion.

(iv) Acts 15³:

declaring the conversion of the Gentiles.

This is the case in which unanimity is most nearly
achieved. In this case it is easier simply to note the
translations which do not use the word *conversion*.
Wicliffe in his first edition used the vivid word *lyvynge*,
the living, the bringing to life of the Gentiles. In his
second edition he altered it to *conversation*, which the
Bishops' Bible followed, but in this case *conversation* is
intended to be the same word as *conversion*, and is simply
the form from the verb *conversari* instead of *convertere*.
Moffatt and Knox both have it that Paul and Barnabas
told that 'the Gentiles were turning to God'. For the

17

translators of the New Testament in Basic English the word *conversion* was not available because it was not included in the agreed basic vocabulary, so they speak of the *salvation* of the Gentiles. Thus even here there is variation, although here we are nearest to agreement.

Of all the translators Moffatt is most sparing in his use of the words convert and conversion, for he only keeps it once, in 1 Timothy 3[6].

We must now try to pin down and to define more closely the meaning of the Greek words which are translated by *convert* and its allied words. We may disregard the passages where the idea of conversion is introduced into the words proselyte (*prosēlutos*), first fruits (*aparchē*), and recent convert (*neophutos*), for the idea there is perfectly clear. In the other cases two words are involved. The commoner is *epistrephein* (Matt 13[15]; Mk 4[12]; Acts 28[27]; Lk 22[32]; Jas 1[19, 20]), with which the word *epistrophē*, translated *conversion* in Acts 15[3], is closely connected. The other word is *strephein*, which in this sense occurs only in Matthew 18[3]. Let us first examine *epistrephein*. In classical and secular Greek *epistrephein* is a common word, and it has no technical religious sense at all.

(i) It is the word for *to turn* in both the transitive and the intransitive senses of the term. It can be used for turning one's back upon someone (Herodotus, 7.141); for turning a ship in the sense of sending it veering off on a fresh tack (Thucydides, 2.90); of making horses wheel round (Plutarch, *Sulla*, 19). In the intransitive sense it is used of turning about, or turning round. It can be used of a ship putting about (Polybius, 1.47.8); of a wild boar turning and rounding on a huntsman to attack him (Xenophon, *On Hunting*, 10.15). It is the common word for the physical act of causing someone or something to turn, or of turning oneself.

(ii) It has one usage which is really a Hebraism. It is used in the sense of returning to do something in the sense of doing it again. If Israel is faithful to God and if the nation repents, 'the Lord will again take delight [literally, will return to take delight] in prospering you, as he took delight in your fathers' (Deut 30⁹). It is said of Manasseh that 'he rebuilt the high places which his father Hezekiah had broken down', where the expression is literally 'returned and rebuilt' (2 Chron 33³). Here the idea is of returning to some previously performed action. The idea is that of doing again.

(iii) But the word is used in a sense other than a physical sense. Both transitively and intransitively it can mean *to turn the mind, the attention, to*. In this sense it has become quite common in later Greek. In the papyri complaint is made against a certain Sarapion that he has paid no attention (*mē epistrepsantos*) to the instructions to sail down (*P. Oxy.*, 3.486.30). It is complained against two brothers that, though they owe money, they do not show the slightest inclination (*kat' ouden epistrephontai*) to repay (B.G.U., 1.36.7). So the word has entered the mental world with the meaning of *turning the attention to*.

(iv) This opens the way to a further series of meanings which move in the direction of the meaning of the word which we are particularly studying. To turn the attention of a person to someone or to something can be to warn him, to correct him, to cause him to repent, and hence to convert him; and to have the attention so turned is to heed, to repent, to take warning, and so to be converted. So Lucian lays down how he thinks history should be written with care and meticulous accuracy, and then he goes on to say: 'I know that I shall not convert very many; some indeed will think me a great nuisance' (*How History must be Written*, 5). Plutarch uses it in the sense of giving heed to a saying (*Alcibiades*, 16). In Judith we have the phrase: 'Now they have returned to God' which is equivalent to 'They have repented' (Jud 5¹⁹). Closest of all to the technical religious sense of the term is an instance in Epictetus. 'What is your opinion of piety and sanctity?' is the question. 'If you wish I shall prove that it is good,' is the answer. And the reply is: 'By all means prove it, that our citizens may be converted (*epistrepsantos*) and may honour the divine one, and at last cease to be indifferent about the things that are of supreme importance' (Epictetus, *Discourses*, 2.20.22).

From this it can be seen that the basic meaning of the word *epistrephein* is a turning round either in the physical or the mental or the spiritual sense of the term; and that thus when the word moves in the world of thought and religion it means a change of outlook and a new direction given to life and to action.

Before we turn to the evidence of the New Testament itself we now go on to look at the use of the verb *strephein*. Its use hardly differs at all from the use of *epistrephein*. Both transitively and intransitively it means to turn. It can be used of the military action of a commander in wheeling his troops into a new line of attack (Xenophon, *The Spartans*, 11.9); of causing the potter's wheel to rotate upon its axis (Sannyrio, 4); of turning a thing upside down—for instance, of the capsizing of a boat by inefficient seamanship (Sophocles, *Antigone*, 717); of turning over the earth by digging

(Xenophon, *Oeconomicus*, 15.15). It can be used of a person turning to or from a thing. It too enters the world of ideas rather than of physical things and it can be used of changing one's attitude. 'Even you would soften [turn to softness] if you knew all' (Sophocles, *Ajax*, 1117).

Once again the basic idea is that of changing the direction either in the physical or the mental sense of the term.

We turn now to the evidence of the New Testament itself. In the New Testament *epistrephein* is used more than thirty-five times:

(i) It is used very rarely in the transitive sense. It is said of John the Baptizer that he will *turn* many of the sons of Israel to the Lord their God (Lk 1, [16, 17]). James speaks of the duty and the privilege of bringing back, turning back, someone who has strayed away (Jas 5[19, 20]).

(ii) It is frequently used in the physical sense of turning or returning. The evil spirit says: 'I will return to my house from which I came' (Matt 12[44]). The parents of Jesus returned into Galilee (Lk 2[39]). At the last time he who is in the field is not to turn back to take his mantle (Matt 24[18]; Mk 13[16]; Lk 17[31]; cp. Matt 10[3]; Lk 8[55], 17[4]; Acts 15[36]; 2 Pet 2[22]; Rev 1[12]).

(iii) It is frequently used of a person turning round. So Jesus, when the woman touched the hem of His garment, turned about in the crowd (Mk 5[30]; cp. Mk 8[33]; Jn 21[20]; Acts 9[40], 16[18]).

(iv) It is most frequently of all used of a mental or a spiritual turn. This is the sense of the word with which we are concerned, although the actual word conversion is very seldom used. 'Repent', says Peter, 'and turn again, that your sins may be blotted out' (Acts 3^{19}). When Peter healed Aeneas, all the residents of Lydda and Sharon saw him, and they turned to the Lord (Acts 9^{35}). During the preaching at Antioch a great number that believed turned to the Lord (Acts 11^{21}). It is Paul's appeal at Lystra that the people should turn from these vain things to a living God (Acts 14^{15}). It is the decision of the Jerusalem Council that the Gentiles who turn to God should not be troubled (Acts 15^{19}). It is Paul's conviction that he is divinely commissioned to open the eyes of the Gentiles that they may turn from darkness to light and from the power of Satan to God (Acts 26^{18}), and that they should repent and turn to God (Acts 26^{20}). When a man turns to the Lord the veil is removed (2 Cor 3^{16}). Paul rejoices that the Thessalonians have turned to God from idols (1 Thess 1^9). In their pre-Christian days Peter's people were straying like sheep, but now they have returned to the Shepherd and the Guardian of their souls (1 Pet 2^{25}).

In almost all these instances it is plain to see that it would be easy to introduce the idea of conversion into the translation of the word.

We now turn to *strephein*.

(i) *Strephein* is used in the literal and the physical sense. Pearls are not to be cast before pigs in case they turn and attack you (Matt 7^6). We turn to the Gentiles, said Paul, when the Jews rejected his message of the gospel (Acts 13^{46}).

(ii) It can be used in the sense of to turn or to change something into. In the Revelation (11^9) the two witnesses have power over the waters to turn them into blood.

(iii) It can be used of mental turning. In their hearts the Israelites turned to Egypt (Acts 7[39]).

(iv) But the characteristic use of this word is of a person turning round. It is used of Mary turning round in the Garden (Jn 20[14, 16]). But, especially in Luke, the word has one consistent use. It would seem that Jesus had a characteristic habit of swinging round and looking at people. 'The Lord turned and looked at Peter' (Lk 22[61]). And this word is used no fewer than nine times of this characteristic movement of Jesus (Matt 9[22], 16[23]; Lk 7[9, 44], 9[55], 10[23], 14[25], 22[61], 23[28]).

(v) This particular use of the word throws special light on two instances of this word, the use in John 12[40] and especially in Matthew 18[3]. In the Authorized Version, Matthew 18[3] is translated: 'Except ye be converted, and become as little children, ye shall not enter into the kingdom of heaven.' In this passage the word which is translated *converted* is exactly the same word and the same tense of the word which is used of Jesus turning round. In the passages in which it is used of Jesus it is the aorist participle *strapheis* which is used. Here it is the aorist tense, *straphēte*. When *strephein* is so used for turning it is middle; that is to say, the verb is passive in form, but active in meaning, as with deponent verbs in Latin. It is therefore quite clear that in the Matthew passage the translation should be active and not passive. It ought to be, not 'Except ye be converted', but 'Unless you turn, unless you change'. Both the word *convert* and the passive use of the word here introduce wrong overtones into the translation. It is not technical conversion which is here being spoken of; it is a turning of the mind so that man's outlook on, and attitude to, life are altered from pride to humility.

23

Before we leave this linguistic side of the investigation, it will be well to go back to the Old Testament and to look at the word from which these New Testament words come. That word is the Hebrew word *shubh*, and *shubh* occurs in the Old Testament no fewer than eleven hundred and forty-six times. Once again all its many and varied meanings are bound together by the idea of turning.

(i) *Shubh* means quite simply to return. So it is said that Abraham returned to his place (Gen 18^{33}).

(ii) It means to turn back. So it is said that Ehud turned back at the sculptured stones near Gilgal (Jdg 3^{19}).

(iii) It means to come back from a foreign land. So it is said that Naomi returned from the land of Moab (Ruth 1^6).

(iv) All these meanings of *shubh* are literal and physical, but it too enters into the realm of the mind and the heart and the spirit. It can be used of the hearts of the people returning to a leader or a king in loyalty renewed. So the fear of Jeroboam is that the hearts of the people may return again to Rehoboam, if they continue to go to Jerusalem to offer sacrifice in the Temple there (1 Kings 12^{27}).

(v) It means to change or alter a course of action. So it is said of Jehoiakim that, after a period of acceptance of the foreign yoke, he turned and rebelled against Nebuchadnezzar (2 Kings 24^1).

(vi) It means to turn from sin. So it is said that if the people turn from sin, God's hand will be stayed, and the threat of disaster will be removed (1 Kings 8^{35}).

(vii) It can mean to be restored. So it is said of the hand of Moses that he put it into his breast and it became leprous, and he put it in again and it was restored as the rest of his flesh (Ex 4⁷).

(viii) And above all, it can mean to return to God. Come, says Hosea, and let us return unto the Lord (Hos 6¹).

Here we have exactly the same basic ideas which we found when we were examining *epistrephein* and *strephein*. The basic idea is that of a turn, a change of direction, a reversal of life.

So, then, the basic fact with which we begin is that conversion is a turning of a man's mind and heart and life in the direction of God.

Chapter II

The Turn of Conversion

A TURN involves two things: it involves a *terminus a quo* and a *terminus ad quem*. It involves a turning *from* something and a turning *towards* something. Let us then see from what and to what Christians did turn in the New Testament narrative.

(i) The essence of the turn of the Christian was that it was a turn towards God. When the residents in Lydda and Sharon saw what Peter had done for Aenesa, *they turned to the Lord* (Acts 9³⁵). As a consequence of the preaching at Antioch a great number that believed *turned to the Lord* (Acts 11²). No extra burdens are to be laid on the Gentiles who *turn to God* (Acts 15¹⁹). Paul's message to the Gentiles is that they should repent and *turn to the Lord* (Acts 26²⁰). Peter's people were straying away but have now *returned to the Shepherd and Guardian of their souls* (1 Pet 2²⁵).

A man may have many attitudes to God. He may be to all intents and purposes almost completely unaware that God exists at all. Even if he is aware that God exists, he may be completely indifferent to God. For him God is not a real factor in life. He may be so concerned with the activities of the world that for long stretches in life he forgets the very existence of God. Centuries ago when Longinus was writing on the Sublime his complaint was that the men of his generation were lost in money-making and pleasure-seeking. 'Inevitably', he said, 'they cease to look up' (Longinus, *On the Sublime*, 44). As Matthew Arnold had it in his poem on *Absence*:

> *But each day brings its petty dust*
> *Our soon-choked souls to fill,*
> *And we forget because we must*
> *And not because we will.*

A man may be evading God. 'The fool says in his heart, There is no God' (Ps 14[1], 53[1]). The fool in the psalm is the *nabal*. He is not the intellectual fool, not the brainless, stupid man; he is the *moral* fool, the man who, in the modern phrase, is playing the fool. His denial of the existence of God is not due to intellectual doubts or to the failure or inability to understand. His denial of the existence of God is due to the fact that he does not wish there to be a God. His denial of the existence of God is nothing other than wishful thinking; it is an evasion of the fact of the existence of God, sometimes conscious, sometimes unconscious. A man may be actively hostile to God. Swinburne spoke of 'The supreme evil—God'. He may be well aware of the existence of God, and yet hate God.

But it may be that there is an attitude to God which is commoner than any of these attitudes. It is an attitude which has, so to speak, many gradations within it. It includes the man who acknowledges the existence of God, but for whom God is on the circumference of life. As Voltaire said of God: 'We nod, but we do not speak.' It is an attitude of a kind of courteous but uninterested indifference. It includes the attitude of the man for whom religion has a real enough compartment in

27

life. He attends his church; he fulfils the conventional obligations to the Church; but none the less religion remains for him a section and compartment of life, which has its own place, but is seldom or never allowed to exceed its place. It includes the man who has what might be called a spasmodic awareness of God, the man who does know times when God is real, but for whom these times are rather the exception than the rule. Such a man in a moment of crisis may indeed turn to God, but in the routine of life and when the sun is shining he can handle life well enough by himself.

The one characteristic of all these attitudes to God is that in none of them is God the steadily dominant factor in life; in none of them does a man live in a permanent awareness of God; in none of them is a man permanently turned in the direction of God; in none of them is God at the centre of life. In real conversion a man is turned round and left permanently facing God. For him the presence of the risen Christ is the very atmosphere of life. He is as much *in Christ*, in Paul's great phrase, as he is in the air which surrounds him and which gives him the breath of life. He can say: 'For me to live is Christ', or, as Moffatt vividly translated it: 'Life means Christ to me' (Phil 2²¹). In real conversion life is no longer an oscillation, but a state in which life is permanently turned towards God.

(ii) Just as the New Testament sees conversion as a turn *towards* God, it sees it as a turn *away* from certain things.

(a) It is a turn away from idols to serve the living and true God (1 Thess 1⁹). It is a turn away from vain things to a living God (Acts 14¹⁵). The Bible is always

28

insistent on the livingness of God and the deadness of all false gods. Isaiah draws his two grimly humorous pictures. He draws the picture of the man forging and casting his idol in the fire and growing weary and thirsty in the process; of the man choosing his piece of wood and with half of it making a fire to cook a meal and to warm himself and with half of it making a god (Isa 44⁹⁻¹⁸). He draws a picture of a god who has to be carried from place to place and who is incapable of any movement for himself, of a god under whose weight his weary worshippers stagger and fall, when they have to carry him away on their shoulders and on their beasts when their enemies invade their city (Isa 46¹⁻⁷).

This is not simply a picture which comes from the days when men did make the images of their gods from wood and stone and metal. It is the picture of an eternal principle. Conversion is the turn of the soul from things to God. A man's god is that to which he gives his life; and conversion is the time when a man gives his life not to material things but to God.

(b) It is a turn from darkness to light, and from the power of Satan to God (Acts 26¹⁸). There are three things here, of which two come from the first of the two phrases.

1. To turn from darkness to light means to turn from ignorance to knowledge. It might well be said that conversion is bound to be due to the realization of what God is really like. If God is no more than indifferent, there is no point in turning to one who in any event does not care. The Stoics insisted that God cannot be God unless He is completely insulated from all feeling and from every emotion; for God to be God no one

29

must be able in any way to influence or to affect Him, for God to be God He can know no love or grief. The Epicureans insisted that if the serenity of God is to be maintained, then God cannot have any interest in the world; for God to have any concern with the world would bring dispeace to His unbroken peace, for concern and serenity are mutually contradictory. There is no point in turning to a god who by his very nature would not even notice if you turned. If God is simply inexorable law, avenging justice, unapproachable holiness, then there is no point in turning to Him. There would be no welcome there; there would be nothing but condemnation and obliteration. The human soul would desire above all things rather to flee in terror from such a god than to turn in hope towards him. We cannot turn to God, unless we know that God is love. Conversion is born from the fact that God wants man to turn to Him; true conversion cannot spring from anything else than the realization of the revelation of the love of God in Jesus Christ.

2. But in biblical thought darkness and light stand not only for ignorance and knowledge; they stand for evil and good. And conversion means the turn of the heart from evil to good. It means a shift of the centre of joy; it means that the soiled and dark things in which a man once found delight now repel him, and that he makes the discovery that purity is more thrilling than sin.

3. But the turn is also from the power of Satan to God. This is the turn from frustration to victory, the turn in which a man ceases to be the slave of sin and becomes the conqueror of sin. It is the discovery that in the power of God the apparently unconquerable power of sin can be overcome.

Chapter III

The Means towards the Change

THE nature of the change of conversion we have seen; we must now go on to see how the change is produced and brought about.

In this change man and God co-operate; we might well say that to produce this change in men God needs the help of men. Of this divine-human co-operation the leaders of the early Church were fully conscious. When Paul and Barnabas returned from the first missionary journey, they declared all that God had done with them (Acts 14^{27}); and when they came to Jerusalem to discuss the situation of the Gentiles, once again they declared all that God had done with them (Acts 15^4). In English *with* has a certain ambiguity. It could mean *using them as an instrument or agent*, as we speak, for instance, of driving in a nail *with* a hammer; but in the Greek there is no ambiguity, for the word for *with* is *meta*, which means *in the company of, in partnership with*. Here we have the great challenge and the privilege of the Christian. The Christian is called upon to be the partner of God in the work of the conversion of men.

(i) This partnership is necessary because the main means of conversion in the early Church was *preaching*. The Gentiles came into the Church because they *heard and believed* (Acts 15^7). We must then look at this preaching which was the means of conversion.

In all this preaching Jesus Christ was uncompromisingly central. 'There is salvation in no one else, for there is no other name under heaven given among men by which we must be saved' (Acts 4¹²). Here is something which to the ancient world was new. There was a certain sublime intolerance in Christianity. Christianity came into a world in which syncretism and religion were to all intents and purposes synonymous. Men had the feeling that no one religion could claim pre-eminence, and that the way to God would best be found in a kind of amalgam of them all. As Symmachus had it: 'There cannot be one way to so great a secret.' As Maximus had it: 'God is a name which all religions share.' It was the uncompromising claim of Christianity, not that all other religions were useless, but that at best they were broken lights, glimpses, fragmentary atoms of knowledge, and that the only full and true revelation of God was in Jesus Christ.

But however fixed the centre of the Christian converting message was, its presentation was widely varied. The early Christian preachers had the will and the ability to begin from where their hearers were. We have three more or less full notes of Paul's preaching material in three different circumstances. First, we have his sermon in the Synagogue at Antioch in Pisidia (Acts 13¹⁶⁻⁴¹). There Paul was preaching to Jews and to God-fearers, and his arsenal was the Old Testament and Jewish faith and hopes. Second, we have his sermon on Mars' Hill in Athens (Acts 17²²⁻³¹), and there he began from Greek religion and philosophy, and cited to the Greeks their own Cleanthes and Aratus. Third, we have a brief record of his appeal at Lystra in remote Lycaonia (Acts 14¹⁵⁻¹⁷), and there he began from natural religion, from God in the events of nature, from truths which even the simplest and most uninstructed mind could see. The preaching which aims at conversion must inescapably begin where a man is before it can bring him to where God wants him to be. The one saving faith can be presented in many ways, and it is a significant fact that Paul did not reject the approach through Scripture, through philosophy, and through natural religion.

This converting message which the preacher brings to men from God is characterized in a variety of ways.

(a) It is good news; it is essentially a gospel (Acts 10^{36}, 14$^{7, 21}$, 15^7, 20^{24}). Whatever may be the perils and the penalties of ignoring it or refusing it, the message itself is such that it must make glad the hearts of men.

(b) It is divinely given; it is the word of God, the word of the Lord (Acts 13^{44}, 17^{13}, 19^{10}). It is the word which comes from God and tells of God. It is not simply a man's opinion; it is the divine message of the divine offer in Jesus Christ.

(c) It is a message of life (Acts 5^{20}). It is designed to enable a man to live with a fulness which has never been in his life before. It is quite wrong to think of Christianity as a limiting and prohibitive thing; it is meant to introduce into life a new spaciousness and power.

(d) It is a message of peace (Acts 10^{36}). In Hebrew thought the basic meaning of *peace* is *right relationships*. It is a message which will put a man into a right relationship with God and with his fellow-men.

(e) It is a message of grace (Acts 14^3, 20$^{24, 32}$). That is to say, it is a message which comes with an offer to man, freely and spontaneously made by God. The New

33

Testament consistently stresses the offer of God at least as much as it does the demand of God.

(*f*) It is a message of salvation (Acts 13²⁶, 16¹⁷). That is to say, it is the message which tells of that which can rescue a man from the situation in which he finds himself in time and in eternity, and which can bring into his life a new welfare and well-being. It must never be forgotten that the word *sōtēria* has a negative and a positive meaning. It was not originally a religious word at all and meant quite simply health and well-being. The soldier Apion writes to his father Epimachus: 'I beg you, my dear father, send me a few lines about your *sōtēria*. Send me a note to tell me how you are' (G. Milligan, *Selections from the Greek Papyri*, 36.13, B.G.U., 423). Health involves on the one side cure of illness and on the other positive well-being. Salvation promises a man escape from his present situation and a new situation in which life is well.

This conversion preaching had certain ever-recurring notes in it:

(*a*) It stresses the crime of the Cross. In every mention of the Cross there come across the centuries two notes in the voices of the early preachers. There is a kind of thrill of staggered horror; they speak like men shocked and aghast in the presence of the supreme crime in history. And there is a kind of blazing accusation of those who were responsible for this crime. 'This Jesus . . . you crucified and killed by the hands of lawless men' (Acts 2²³). 'You denied the Holy and Righteous One, and asked for a murderer to be granted to you, and killed the Author of Life' (Acts 3¹⁴, ¹⁵). 'The Righteous One whom you betrayed and murdered' (Acts 7⁵²; cp. 4¹⁰, 5³⁰, 10³⁹, 13²⁷⁻⁹). Here men are confronted with what Carlyle called 'the infinite damnability of sin'. Here there is set before men the destructive and murderous and blasphemous power of sin that they may recoil in horror from it.

(b) It stresses the glory of the Resurrection. Again and again the crime of man in the Crucifixion and the power of God in the Resurrection are juxtaposed. 'The God of our fathers raised Jesus whom you killed by hanging him on a tree' (Acts 5^{30}). 'They put him to death by hanging him on a tree, but God raised him on the third day' (Acts $10^{39, \ 40}$). The very essence of apostolic preaching was the Resurrection; both in Jerusalem and in Athens this was the one salient thing that struck men's minds about the Christian preaching. 'With great power the apostles gave their testimony to the resurrection of the Lord Jesus' (Acts 4^{33}; cp. 4^2, 13^{30}, $17^{18, \ 31}$, 25^{19}, 26^{23}).

It is never to be forgotten that the conversion preaching of the early Church was centred every bit as much on the Resurrection as it was on the Cross. It may well be that one of the supreme failures of modern preaching is that it has often confined the message of the Resurrection to Easter Day, while to the early Church it was the theme of every sermon that they preached on every day. They consistently presented men, not only with a crucified Saviour, but with a Risen and Ever-present Lord.

(c) It stresses the fulfilment of prophecy. This is the theme of sermon after sermon in the Book of Acts (2^{17-31}, $3^{18, \ 25}$, $4^{11, \ 25, \ 26}$, 8^{30-5}, 10^{43}, $13^{16-23, \ 33-7}$, $13^{41, \ 47}$, 15^{15-17}, 17^3, $26^{22, \ 23}$, 28^{25-7}).

It may be that this is an argument which has lost a very great deal of its force, because we are no longer able to interpret the Old Testament as the early Christians interpreted it. But this argument had one great value, and still has one great value.

It had the value that it was the one weapon which would convince the Jews. The Jews had to be convinced that Jesus was the Messiah, and there was no other way of really convincing them than out of their own Scriptures. This was in fact the supreme weapon in the Christian armoury in controversy with the Jews.

It has this supreme value that it shows the whole scheme of salvation, not as a desperate emergency measure, which God adopted when all else was lost, but as the unfolding of the eternal plan of God. Crime of man the Cross may be, act of the mind of God it certainly is. 'This Jesus, delivered up according to the definite plan and foreknowledge of God, you crucified and killed by the hands of lawless men' (Acts 2^{23}). Somehow even the terrible sin of man was integrated into the plan of God. The love on the Cross is not what God suddenly became but what God always was and is and ever shall be.

(d) The conversion preaching came with a double offer. It came with the offer of the forgiveness of sins and the gift of the Spirit (Acts 2^{38}, 3^{19}, $5^{31, \ 32}$, 8^{15-17}, 9^{17}, 10^{44-7}, 11^{15}, 13^{38}, 15^{8}). That is to say, it came with the offer of release from the past and strength for the future. It offered a man the love of God to blot out the past, and the strength of God to make new the future.

(e) Finally, the conversion preaching came with an unmistakable threat. It placed fairly and squarely before men the consequences of refusing the offer of God in Jesus Christ, and the certainty of judgement ($3^{22, \ 23}$, 7^{51-3}, 10^{42}, $13^{40, \ 46}$, $17^{30, \ 31}$, 18^{6}, 24^{25}, 28^{28}). The early preaching confronted men with the same choice as that with which the inner voice confronted John Bunyan: 'Wilt thou leave thy sins and go to heaven, or wilt thou have thy sins and go to hell?' The early preachers were offering men the greatest gift in the world, but that very offer brought with it the greatest responsibility in the world. It has been said that the Bible centres upon man at the cross-roads. The continual challenge of the Bible is: 'Choose ye!' Sometimes Dr Johnson's friends were disturbed by the forthright violence of his conversation, and there were some who would have had him gentler and milder; but one who knew him well and loved him much declared that, even if she had been able, she would never have turned the tiger into the tabby-cat. The early preachers never shirked the task of confronting men with the choice between Heaven and Hell, between life and death.

(ii) But there was another kind of approach which the early preachers, and especially Paul, consistently used. It may be said that the kind of preaching which so far we have been outlining was proclamation. It was the clear and plain statement of the Christian message and of the Christian claim. But the early preachers repeatedly used not only the monologue, but also the dialogue. Much of their most valuable and effective work was done in discussion and debate. It was Stephen's skill in debate which aroused the frustrated anger of the Jews, and which made them resort to slander when they were defeated in argument (Acts 6⁹⁻¹⁴). Paul's first essay in communication was to enter into debate with the Jews in Damascus and to rout them in debate, as he did also in Jerusalem (Acts 9²², ²⁹). It is significant to note how often the word *argue* is used in connexion with Paul. In Thessalonica for three weeks he argued with the Jews from the Scriptures (Acts 17$^{2, 3}$). In Corinth he argued in the Synagogue every Sabbath (Acts 18^4). In Ephesus he went into the Synagogue and argued with the Jews (Acts 18^{19}). For three months he argued and pleaded about the kingdom in the Synagogue, and, when he was ejected from the Synagogue he continued to carry on his public debate in the lecture hall of Tyrannus every day (Acts 19$^{8, 9}$). He argued with Felix and with the Jews in Rome (Acts 24^{25}, 28^{23}).

There is one very significant passage about this method of dispute and debate. It is in connexion with Apollos, that skilled Alexandrian scholar and interpreter and debater. When Apollos arrived in Corinth, 'he greatly helped those who through grace had believed, for he powerfully confuted the Jews in public, showing by the scriptures that the Christ was Jesus' (Acts 18$^{27, 28}$). Here is the idea that argument is the ally of grace, that that which has been received through grace must be buttressed and supported and developed by the application to it of the skill of the mind.

It can never be said of the early Church that its preachers depended on anything like a kind of mass emotionalism. It may be that one of the greatest failures of modern evangelism to produce any permanent and lasting effect has been due to nothing other than its suspicion of anything like an intellectual approach to faith and its dependence on emotionalism. J. S. Whale has said that it is a moral duty to be intelligent. E. F. Scott has said that more often than we realize the failure of religion as a moral power has been due to nothing other than intellectual sloth. And long before this Peter had said to his people: 'Always be prepared to make a defence to anyone who calls you to account for the hope that is in you' (1 Pet 3^{15}).

It may well be that the greatest need of the Church today in its task of conversion is the development of what we might call 'educational evangelism', and the discovery that the monologue of the pulpit must be supported by the dialogue of personal discussion. The day when the sole instrument of evangelism was the mass meeting is necessarily past; and now there is laid upon the individual Christian the absolute necessity of knowing his own faith so that he can intelligently commend it to others. The Church is paying heavily today for its neglect of the teaching ministry, and, if the example of the early Church is to be followed, that teaching evangelism must be made a main instrument in the work of conversion.

(iii) According to the story in Acts, a main instrument in the converting work of the early preachers and apostles was the healing work which they were able to do. It was the healing of the lame man at the Beautiful Gate of the Temple which set Jerusalem in a ferment and which the Jewish leaders were quite unable to deny (Acts 3$^{1-10}$, 4$^{16, 21, 30}$). It was to benefit from their healing ministry that the people flocked to the apostles (Acts 5$^{12-16}$). Philip exercised this power in Samaria (Acts 8$^{6, 7}$); Peter healed Aeneas and Dorcas (Acts 9$^{32-42}$); In Cyprus, in Iconium, in Lystra, in Philippi, in Ephesus, in Malta, Paul exercised this healing power (Acts 13^{12}, 14$^{3, 8-10}$, 16^{18}, 19$^{11-20}$, 28$^{1-10}$).

David Smith quotes a saying that in those days these apostolic miracles were the bells which called people into the Church. It has been held that there was at that time a special and non-recurring period of power in the Church, divinely sent and supplied by God, so that the claims of the Church might be demonstrably and unmistakably authenticated.

It must be remembered that in that ancient world this kind of thing was much more common than it is today. Suetonius, for instance, tells how there were brought to Vespasian, the Roman Emperor, a man who was blind and a man who was lame. At their request, Vespasian spat into the eyes of the blind man and touched the leg of the lame man with his heel, and they were both healed (Suetonius, *Vespasian*, 7). It was told that when Hadrian was dying an old blind man from Pannonia came to him and touched him and received his sight (*The History of the Caesars, Hadrian*, 25). It is beyond doubt that many people were cured from their diseases in the temples of Aesculapius, the god of healing. It may well be that the explanation is that a great many illnesses in ancient times—as is still true today—were psychological in their origin, and in an age when miracles were expected miracles happened, for it is always to a man according to his faith.

The really important thing is not to discuss whether these miracles really happened or not, or, if they happened, to argue how they happened. The really important thing is that in those early days the pagans saw in Christianity and in the Church a power that could cope with and mend the human situation. They saw in Christianity a power which they did not possess —and they wanted it. It will always be true that the outsider will have no use for an alleged faith which is demonstrably ineffective. Long ago Nietschze, the atheist philosopher, issued the challenge: 'Show me that you are redeemed and then I will believe in your Redeemer.' The greatest converting influence of all is a life which clearly and obviously is possessed of a power which can cope with the human situation in all its problems, in all its tragedy, and in all its pain.

(iv) This leads us naturally and inevitably to the next weapon in the converting ministry of the Church—the personal witness of the Christian. This idea of personal testimony has three forms in the converting ministry of the early Church.

(a) The early preachers testified to the faith which they held and to the experience which they had gone through (Acts 2⁴⁰, 8²⁵, 10⁴², 18⁵, 20²¹, 20²⁴, 26²²). They were for ever commending to others that which they themselves had personally experienced.

(b) The early preachers witnessed to facts which they personally knew to be true. 'This Jesus God raised up, and of that we all are witnesses' (Acts 2³²). Paul testified to the Jews that the Christ was Jesus (Acts 18⁵; cp. 3¹⁵, 5³², 10³⁹, 13³¹). This function of witness to known facts was a paramount apostolic duty. The commission of the Church was: 'You shall be my witnesses in Jerusalem and in all Judaea and in Samaria and to the end of the earth' (Acts 1⁸). The commission to Paul is: 'You will be a witness to him to all men of what you have seen and heard' (Acts 22¹⁵; cp. 26¹⁶).

But the whole point of this witness is that conversion preaching is not aiming at transmitting certain facts; it is aiming at communicating an experience. It is in effect saying: 'I have found this to be true; I personally guarantee its truth. Will you try it for yourself and see?'

(c) But, clearly, the best of all witness is not the

witness of words, but the witness of life. And it was here that the Christian witness was most effective of all. It was particularly effective in the days of martyrdom. As H. B. Workman put it: 'Every martyr's death was an emphatic *credo*, uttered in a language that all could understand' (*Persecution in the Early Church*, 346). Justin Martyr writes:

I myself, when I was contented with the doctrines of Plato, and heard the Christians slandered, yet saw them fearless of death, and of everything men count terrible, felt that it was impossible that these men could be living, as was reputed, in wickedness and mere pleasure (*Second Apology*, 12).

Workman tells of a young officer attached to the court of Galerius. He was deeply impressed by the courage of the martyrs at Nicomedeia. He went to the Christians and asked them the secret of their courage. He was instructed in the Christian faith. On the next occasion when Christians were examined, he stepped forward and requested Galerius to add his name to theirs. 'Are you mad?' demanded Galerius. 'Do you wish to throw away your life?' 'I am not mad,' was the answer. 'I was mad once, but am now in my right mind.' And so he died.

The Christian witness to the Christian experience, the Christian personal guarantee of the facts, the Christian love for all men, the Christian courage in martyrdom were all parts of the converting ministry of the Church. It will always remain true that people will look twice at a belief which makes a man a man of love and courage; and it will also always remain true that people will not spare a second glance for a faith which appears to have no effect whatever on the man who professes it.

(v) Finally, we may note the place of the Scriptures as a converting instrument in the early days of the Church. It is true that the Scriptures became an even more influential medium of conversion after New Testament times, but even within the period of Acts they played their part. We find that, when Philip approached him, the Ethiopian eunuch was reading the prophet Isaiah (Acts 8²⁸). We find that the courteous Beroeans examined the Scriptures daily to check and to investigate the message that Paul brought to them (Acts 17¹¹). And there is no doubt that the process of debate and argument which we have already seen to be so important must have been based on the examination of the Scriptures and the Christian interpretation of them.

In the history of the early Church we find three outstanding instances in which the converting instrument was the Scriptures, and in each case the Scriptures of the Old Testament. The first is the case of Tatian. Tatian had deeply studied philosophy; he had been admitted to the Mysteries; and he had investigated all religious rites. Then he goes on:

Retiring by myself, I sought how I might be able to discover the truth, and, while I was giving my most earnest attention to this matter, I happened to meet with certain barbaric writings, too old to be compared with the opinions of the Greeks, and too divine to be compared with their errors; and I was led to put faith in these by the unpretending cast of their language, the inartificial character of the writers, the foreknowledge displayed of future events, the excellent quality of the precepts, and the declaration of the government of the universe as centred in one Being (*Against the Nations*, 29).

43

For Tatian the Scriptures of the Old Testament were the end of the search for truth.

The second is the case of Theophilus of Antioch. Theophilus too was a man of wide knowledge; he too had been an unbeliever like the Autolycus to whom he writes. He tells of his search for truth, and then he goes on:

At the same time I met with the sacred scriptures of the holy prophets, who also by the Spirit of God foretold the things that have already happened, just as they came to pass, and the things now occurring as they are now happening, and things future in the order in which they shall be accomplished (*To Autolycus*, 1.14).

Theophilus too found in the Scriptures that which he had sought for elsewhere, but had never found.

The third is the case of Athenagoras. Athenagoras was one of the great Greek pagan scholars. He was an authority on Plato and the head of the Academic School of philosophy. He may well have been the Athenagoras to whom Boethus dedicated his book on *Difficult Sentences in Plato*. Almost all that we know about him is contained in an extract from the *Christian History* of Philip of Side. Philip tells us that Athenagoras became a Christian while still wearing the saffron robe, which was the garb of the philosopher. His coming to Christianity was dramatic indeed. Philip says of him: 'Before Celsus he had planned to write against the Christians, but, reading the Holy Scriptures to make his attack the more telling, he was so won over by the Holy Spirit as to become, like the great Paul, a teacher and not a persecutor of the faith he was attacking (J. H. Crehan, *Athenagoras*, Ancient Christian Writers'

Series, p. 4). Athenagoras read the Bible to destroy it, and was in the end converted by it.

Scripture was one of the great converting influences in the history of the Church.

So then the great converting influences in the early Church were the preaching of the Christian message with Jesus Christ as the centre of it, the reasoned presentation of the Christian faith in argument and in debate, the argument from the fulfilment of prophecy, the events which showed the reservoir of power for life which Christianity was able to tap, the personal witness of the Christian, and the self-evidencing power of Scripture.

Chapter IV

The Demand from the Convert

THERE can be many reactions to an invitation and to any offer, and there were many reactions to the offer which the Christian preachers brought to men. There was stubborn disbelief, as at Ephesus (Acts 19⁹). There was murderous rage, as on the part of the orthodox leaders of the Jews (Acts 5³³). There was opposition and abuse, as in the case of Corinth (Acts 18⁶). There was bitter jealousy from the Synagogue Jews (Acts 13⁴⁵, 17⁵). This reaction is little to be wondered at. Round each synagogue there had gathered a number of Gentiles, who were attracted by the Jewish worship of one God in contrast to the many gods of paganism, and by the purity of the Jewish ethic in contrast to the immoralities of paganism. These Gentiles were the God-fearers; they did not go the length of accepting circumcision and the whole Jewish law, as the proselytes did, but they were on the verge of Judaism. It was precisely amongst them that Paul was most successful of all (Acts 13⁴³, 17⁴, ¹⁷), and the Jews bitterly resented what they regarded as the stealing and the seducing of possible converts to the Jewish faith. In their jealous resentment, the Jews did everything they could to poison the minds of the authorities against Christianity. There was the reaction of argument and dispute (Acts 6⁹, 9²², ²⁹), but this was no bad thing, for he who is prepared to argue may just possibly be convinced. There was the reaction of academic interest, as in the case of the cultured population of Athens (Acts 17[18]). There was the reaction of alarm, as in the case of Felix (Acts 24[25]). There was the reaction of the sudden realization of the crime of the Cross, as in the case of the Jews of Jerusalem who were cut to the heart when they heard the message of Peter (Acts 2[37]). And there was the reaction of the open and the receptive heart as in the case of Lydia in Philippi (Acts 16[14]). The Christian message provoked different reactions in different hearts.

What, then, is the saving reaction of real and true conversion?

(i) The first demand that the early preachers made was the demand for repentance. It is Paul's message to Jew and to Gentile alike that they should repent and turn to God (Acts 26[20]). God now commands all men everywhere to repent, said Paul in his sermon at Athens (Acts 17[30]; cp. 2[38], 3[19], 5[31], 8[22], 20[21]).

What, then, is this repentance? Of the centrality of its place in the Christian life there is no doubt. Tertullian wrote: 'Penitence is life, since it is preferred to death. Rush upon it, grasp it as a shipwrecked man grasps the aid of a plank. . . . Penitence and full confession are the two Pharos lights of human salvation' (*Concerning Penitence*, 3.9). In actual fact the message of the early preachers was the repetition of the message of Jesus: 'The time is fulfilled, and the kingdom of God is at hand; repent, and believe the gospel' (Mk 1[15]). Let us then try to define more closely what repentance means.

(a) The word for *penitence* or *repentance* is *metanoia*, and the word for *to repent* is *metanoein*. The meaning of *metanoia* is clear; it means an *after-thought*. *Meta* is *afterwards* and *noia* is a *thought*. It is the exact opposite of *pronoia*, which means *forethought*, and the Greek moralists said that a wise man would always use *pronoia*, and then *metanoia* would be unnecessary. Originally and by derivation, *metanoia* simply meant the condition in which a man had second thoughts about something.

(*b*) Now, an afterthought, a second thought, is often a *changed* thought. It is often the realization of error and mistake. It is the awakened awareness that some action or some decision was not as it should have been.

(*c*) So then *metanoia* comes to involve not only a new judgement on some previous action, but also regret and sorrow for it. Here, then, is the meaning of repentance. Repentance is the awakened awareness of past sin.

Having got this length in the elucidation of the meaning of repentance, two further things must clearly be seen:

1. Repentance is not simply regret for the consequences of some action. It, as we shall immediately see, certainly involves that. But it must involve very much more. If repentance was simply regret for the consequences of some action, it might well mean that a man would do the same thing again, if he could be sure that this time he would escape the consequences of his action. That kind of regret is not so much regret for the action itself, as regret for having been found out. In many cases a man is not so much sorry that he did a thing as sorry for the mess into which it has brought him. If he could escape the consequences, or if he could arrange to do the same thing without the

consequences, he would quite certainly do it again. Repentance is a genuine sorrow for the wrong thing; a genuine shame for the feelings and the motives which inspired it; a genuine discovery that the thing was wrong in the sight of God. 'Penitence', said Tertullian, 'is a certain passion of the mind which comes from disgust at some previous feeling' (*Concerning Penitence*, 1). We must make a clear distinction between sorrow for the consequences of an action, and sorrow for the action itself.

2. So, then, repentance is a kind of self-disgust. How is this self-disgust to be brought home to a man? There are two ways to this shame. First, it is perfectly true that the sight of the consequences of some sin may indeed waken penitence in the true sense of the term. Certain American courts devised a very effective punishment for those who had been guilty of reckless or careless or drunken driving of a motor-car. In certain American courts, in addition to a fine or a prison sentence, a guilty driver is compelled to spend a decreed time in the casualty ward of a hospital, so that he may see just what kind of damage such driving can do. Now, penitence may well be awakened when a son or daughter sees the pain in a parent's eyes, or when he sees the tragedy in which he has involved someone who is the victim of his sin. This is certainly true. But, second, the New Testament says that not only salvation, but also penitence is the gift of Jesus Christ. God has exalted Jesus at His right hand as Leader and Saviour to give repentance to Israel and forgiveness of sins (Acts 5[31]). So, then, Jesus is as much the agent of repentance as He is of forgiveness. How? There are two ways in which Jesus is the agent of repentance.

49

First, the Cross is the proof of the terrible things that sin can do. Sin in its terrible destructive power could and did take the loveliest life that was ever lived and tried to break it for ever on a cross. There is nothing in the universe which shows the consequences of sin like the Cross.

Second, realization not infrequently comes from comparison. A thing may be seen in its true light when it is set beside that which at its best it ought to be. So when a man's life is set in the light of Christ's life a man may see with cruel but salutary clarity the ugliness of his own life.

It could be said that penitence comes in the last analysis from seeing sin as God sees it.

(ii) The second demand that the early preachers made was the demand for baptism. Peter's invitation was: 'Repent and be baptized' (Acts 2^{38}, $8^{12, \ 36-8}$, 9^{18}, 10^{48}, 16^{15}, 18^{8}, 22^{16}). In the early Church it was the universal practice of the Church that the new convert was immediately baptized. It is necessary that we should try to understand the place of baptism in the converting ministry and the conversion experience of the early Church.

(a) Baptism was always adult baptism; it is not until much later than this that child baptism became the practice of the Church.

(b) Whether a man came into the Church from Judaism or Hellenism, baptism would be to him a perfectly normal and customary method of initiation with which he was perfectly familiar, and which in some other form he had very probably already experienced.

Every Jew knew well the many purificatory washings

that the ceremonial side of his religion involved (e.g. Lev 15). If he was a proselyte and a convert to Judaism, baptism was in fact one of the three things which formed the entry to the Jewish faith. The other two were circumcision and sacrifice. There were indeed certain liberal rabbis who would have said that baptism in itself was enough. If he was a searching and seeking Greek, the likelihood is that he would already have sought God in some mystery religion and there too initiatory cleansing by baptism was the practice. All Mithraic chapels were in fact built with the bath in which baptism was administered. To a man of the ancient world baptism was neither new nor strange nor embarrassing. It was perfectly familiar.

(c) Since the man to be baptized was an adult, baptism could be very much more of a deliberate action and very much more of a personal experience than it ever can be in the case of child baptism. On the one side, baptism was a perfectly deliberate publicizing of a far-reaching act of decision. It was a deliberate action in which a man left one religion to enter another, in which he said farewell to one way of life and committed himself to another. Baptism was something which marked a clean cut and a definite dividing-line in life. It was the public confession of a radical change which a man had deliberately chosen and to which he pledged himself. It was in fact nothing less than the man's public affirmation that his conversion was real.

(d) But baptism was not only an action; it was also an experience. It was in fact a double experience in which two things came together.

1. There is something else which is consistently connected with repentance and with baptism, and that is

the experience of the forgiveness of sins. 'Repent therefore, and turn again, that your sins may be blotted out' (Acts 3[19]). Through Jesus Christ God offers to Israel repentance and the forgiveness of sins (Acts 5[31]). 'Repent and be baptized every one of you in the name of Jesus Christ for the forgiveness of your sins' (Acts 2[38]). 'Rise and be baptized, and wash away your sins calling on his name' (Acts 22[16]). Baptism was not by sprinkling, but by immersion, and the symbolism of baptism is peculiarly fitted to signify the cleansing of forgiveness. The process must have been as follows. In the preaching of the Christian message a man was offered the forgiveness of sins; in his heart was the desire to accept it; and in the moment of baptism with its physical cleansing the spiritual cleansing also suddenly became a reality to him. Baptism was a dramatic action which turned a promise into a reality.

2. There is something still further which is consistently connected with baptism, and that is the gift of the Holy Spirit. The invitation of Peter ran in full: 'Repent and be baptized every one of you in the name of Jesus Christ for the forgiveness of your sins; and you shall receive the gift of the Holy Spirit' (Acts 2[38], 8[16, 17]). It was when the experience of the Holy Spirit did not come that there was something inadequate about baptism (Acts 19[1-7]).

This experience manifested itself in speaking with tongues (Acts 10[46]). The particular manifestation is not in itself important; what is important is that it was clear that into the life of the converted person there had come a power which was more than of this world.

In the ancient world baptism and conversion were intimately and even indissolubly connected. Baptism was the moment of declaration on the part of the convert that he had entered into a new life, and it was the means whereby the forgiveness of sins was personally appropriated and the power of the Holy Spirit entered into the convert.

(iii) The third thing that the early preachers demanded was belief. It may well be said that the demand for belief was the central and all-important demand. 'What must I do to be saved?' was the question of the gaoler at Philippi. And Paul's answer was: 'Believe in the Lord Jesus Christ, and you will be saved' (Acts 16$^{30, 31}$). The coming into the Church of the early converts is regularly described in terms of belief. So in Jerusalem, many of those who heard the word believed (Acts 4^4). In Samaria they believed Philip as he preached the good news (Acts 8^{12}, 9^{42}, 11^{21}, 13$^{12, 48}$, 14^1, 17$^{2, 34}$, 18^8). In very many of these cases it would be quite possible in paraphrasing the passage to substitute the words *be converted* for the word *believe*, for essentially to believe and to be converted are one and the same thing. What, then, were the early preachers demanding when they demanded belief?

First of all, it is to be noted that this word *believe* is the verb of which the word *faith* is the noun (*pisteuō* and *pistis*). To believe and to have faith are the same. So then we could just as well put the question in the form: What is faith?

(*a*) Faith is the settled conviction that certain things are true. It is the conviction that Jesus Christ showed men what God is like, and that He by His life and His death made possible a new relationship between man and God, a relationship in which estrangement has turned into reconciliation. Without this conviction,

53

faith cannot even make a beginning. Faith is based on the discovery of the possibility of a new relationship to God made possible by Jesus Christ.

(b) But although faith begins with this knowledge, faith is much more than knowledge. Knowledge in itself need have no effect upon life. As James said, the demons are intellectually convinced that God is one, but they remain demons for all that (Jas 2^{19}). Their intellectual knowledge of the nature of God did not in any way alter them. Faith is not only the knowledge of the facts; it is the committal of life to the facts.

Let us take an analogy. I believe that the square on the hypotenuse of a right-angled triangle is equal to the sum of the squares on the other two sides; but it makes not the slightest difference to me. It is a piece of intellectual knowledge of the truth of which I am not in doubt, but which has no effect on my life whatsoever. I accept it, but I am not in any sense committed to it. On the other hand, I believe that six and six make twelve, and because of that I will resolutely refuse to pay one shilling and threepence for two sixpenny bars of chocolate. Here is a fact, my belief in which affects and even dominates my life. It is a fact which has a daily effect on my life. I accept it, and I am committed to it in action. This is exactly the difference between knowledge and faith. Knowledge is intellectual acceptance by the mind; faith is total commitment by the whole personality. To put this in its distinctively religious sense—faith is the decision to live on the assumption that the commands of Jesus Christ are absolutely binding and the promises of Jesus Christ are absolutely true.

(c) But once we have reached this stage a further fact

becomes clear. This commitment which we have just been describing is ultimately not committal to a set of facts; it is committal to a person. This is so because no one would ever commit himself to these facts, unless he had complete confidence in the person who made them known to him. If we have to commit our whole lives, and indeed our eternal destiny to certain beliefs about God, then it is obvious that we must have the most complete trust and confidence in the person who taught us these things, and who, as it were, claims to speak for God. Since this is so, faith ultimately becomes nothing other than committal in trust to Jesus Christ. And we shall be right to stress the fact that the New Testament does not say, 'I know *what* I have believed', but 'I know *whom* I have believed'. In the last analysis, faith is commitment to Jesus Christ.

So then we may say that conversion begins with repentance, is confirmed in baptism, and is founded from beginning to end on commitment in trust to Jesus Christ.

Chapter V

The Obligations of the Convert

IT is clear that when a man becomes a convert to the Christian faith there must be certain changes in his life. In other words, there are certain obligations laid upon the convert. We must look first at what we might call the general obligation, and then we will go on to look at the particular and practical aspects of it.

(i) The general obligation is laid down in one of the very commonest words by which a Christian is described. Again and again in the Authorized Version the Christians are called *saints*. So Paul writes to the saints in Rome, the saints in Achaia, the saints at Philippi and the saints at Colosse (Rom 1⁷; 2 Cor 1¹; Phil 1¹; Col 1²). The word *saint* is nowadays an unfortunate translation, because it suggests the kind of figure which we commonly see in a stained-glass window; it suggests a piety and an otherworldliness, which the majority of people do not desire, and of which they do not think themselves capable. They have the feeling that, if Christianity demands that a man should be a saint in the sense in which they recognize the word, Christianity is not for them.

The word involved is *hagios*, and it has never been an easy word to translate. From Wicliffe to the present day there have been at least six different translations of it. Wicliffe himself translated it *holy men*, a translation which Ferrar Fenton followed by translating it *the holy*. It was with Tyndale that the translation *saints* came in, and it was followed by the Great Bible, the Geneva Bible, the Bishops' Bible, the Rheims Bible, the Authorized, the Revised, and the Revised Standard versions. Of the modern translators, Moffatt and Knox both retained *saints*. Weymouth, Goodspeed, Kingsley Williams, and the New English Bible all translate *God's people*. The Twentieth Century New Testament has *Christ's people*. The Amplified New Testament has *saints*, but amplifies into *God's consecrated people*. And, lastly, J. B. Phillips tries to solve the problem by quite simply using the word *Christian* as the equivalent of *hagios*.

The key to the interpretation of this word comes from two uses of it. First, it is the characteristic adjective to describe God. 'I the Lord your God am holy' (Lev 11[44, 45], 19[2], 20[26]). God is supremely the Holy One. Second, it is equally the characteristic word to describe the nation of Israel. In the passages which we have cited it is laid down that they must be holy because God is holy. 'You shall be holy, for I the Lord your God am holy' (Lev 19[2]). Israel is specifically and uniquely *ho hagios laos*, the holy people.

This is to say that this word *hagios*, which in the New Testament describes the Christian, in the Old Testament is the standard word for *holy* (in Hebrew, *kadosh*), and the word which specially describes God and the nation of Israel. What then is the basic idea behind it? The basic idea of both *hagios* and *kadosh* is that of *difference*. That which is holy is different from ordinary things. The Sabbath is holy because it is different from other days; the Temple is holy because it is different

57

from other buildings; Israel is holy because it is different from other nations; God is supremely the Holy One because he is the Wholly Other, different in his being from men. So then the Christian is *hagios*, and that is to say there is laid upon the convert the necessity of being *different*. The life of the convert is not simply a continuation of the life that he has been living; it is not even an improvement and an amendment of the life that he has been living. It involves something much more radical than that. The very terms in which it is described vividly show the radical nature of the change. It is a rebirth (Jn 3³). 'You have been born anew' (1 Pet 1²³). It is a death and a resurrection in which a man becomes dead to sin and alive to God (Rom 6¹¹), a participation in the death and the resurrection of Jesus Christ. It is not simply a recreation, it is a new creation. 'If anyone is in Christ, he is a new creation' (2 Cor 5¹⁷). It is not the kind of change that circumcision or uncircumcision can bring about; it is the kind of change that only a new act of creation can produce (Gal 6¹⁵). So then the convert has entered into a life which is radically different. The strongest condemnation of so many alleged Christians lies precisely in the fact that there is no discernible difference between them and the man who makes no claims at all to being a Christian. Men can never be moved to desire what appears to be merely an ineffective and optional extra to life. This essential difference is at once an essential part of the converted life and the converting life.

But wherein is that difference expressed? It is certainly not expressed in withdrawal from life. The saints, the different ones, are the saints at Philippi and at Colosse (Phil 1¹; Col 1²). The difference is to be expressed in involvement and not in detachment. The finest flower of the Christian life is not the life of the monk, the nun, the hermit, withdrawn into the monastery, the convent, the desert. To call such people 'religious' in a kind of technical sense of the term is the very reverse of New Testament teaching. The difference must be expressed, not in an increasing detachment from life, but in an increasing involvement and identification with life. Conversion will involve the awakening to the obligation to be involved in all the affairs which affect the lives of men. The unconverted man may remain comfortably detached, and may leave the work to others; the converted man will know that the very fact that he is a Christian necessarily involves him in politics, in local government, in his trade union or professional association. Conversion implies obligation to involvement, for it is in involvement that the change in life has to be expressed.

But, given this involvement, wherein is this difference expressed? Paul uses two *in's*, a fact which for some curious reason nearly all the translations obscure. Paul writes to the saints *in Christ Jesus* who are *in Philippi* (*en Christō Iesou, en Philippois*: Phil 1¹; cp. Col 1²). The English translations by rendering *at* Philippi obscure the play on words which is in the Greek. So then the convert is in Philippi, but he is also in Christ Jesus, and it is just there that the difference is expressed.

The phrase in Christ, or in Christ Jesus, is characteristic of Paul. What does it mean? Harnack has said that the only parallel is the way in which we speak of being *in the air*. Unless the air is in us, and unless we are in the air, we die. The air is the atmosphere in which we live, and, if we are removed from it we die. To be divorced from the air is to be divorced from life. So, then, we may put it in this way—Jesus Christ is the atmosphere in whom the Christian lives. There is between him and Jesus Christ an inseparable and an indissoluble connexion. The Christian is never unaware of the presence of Jesus Christ; he never forgets that Jesus Christ is the spectator of all that he does and the hearer of all that he says; he never thinks of himself as attempting or approaching any task alone; he never thinks of taking any decision or arriving at any conclusion without referring the matter to Jesus Christ. His whole life is linked inseparably to the risen and the living and the ever-present Christ. This is the criterion of difference. The Christian is a Christ-filled man living in a Christ-filled world.

Here then is the general obligation of the convert. He is under the obligation to be different; that difference is to be expressed in a deeper and deeper involvement in the human situation in which he finds himself; the criterion of that difference is that he is in Christ just as much as he is in the atmosphere which gives him physical life.

(ii) But this general obligation issues in certain particular obligations. There is first of all the ethical obligation. The New Testament is insistent that not only must a man repent, but that he must also perform deeds worthy of repentance (Acts 26[20]). It cannot be too often said that, although the New Testament never says that a man can be saved *by* works, it always insists that a man is saved *for* works; and any conversion which does not produce a moral and ethical effect upon a man's life and character is not a real conversion at all.

It is characteristic of the letters of Paul that they practically all culminate in an ethical section (Rom 12; 1 Cor 6^{18-20}; Gal 5^{16-24}; Eph 6^{1-9}; Phil $4^{8, 9}$; Col 3^{18}, 4^6; 1 Thess 5^{1-22}; 2 Thess 3^{1-15}). A new chastity, a new purity, a new beauty, a new quality of caring must be an essential part of the result of any conversion experience. The man who is in Christ must be increasingly Christlike. No man can in the end prove that he loves God in any other way than by loving his fellow men.

(iii) It is not possible to leave this matter of the ethical demand of conversion without adding something to it. Simply to insist that conversion brings with it an insistent ethical demand might well leave a man in a state of tension and apprehension, and of discouragement and even despair. There is in the life of the convert an unquestioned ethical demand, but there is also an unquestioned peace. 'We have peace with God through our Lord Jesus Christ' (Rom 5^1). How can there be at one and the same time the great demand and the great peace? The union of the peace and of the demand comes from two facts.

(a) The ethical obligation does not come from a demand to satisfy law; it comes from the necessity to respond to love. The ethical demand comes not from fear of breaking the law, but from the conviction that a man must be prepared to sweat his very heart out to seek to deserve the love with which he has been loved. The motive of any action makes all the difference to the character of the action. If a man is good only because he sees a law which bids him to be good, and a law which he breaks at his peril, then his goodness is the result of fear, and fear is the great creator of tension. But if a man is good because he feels that the miraculous privilege of being loved will not allow him to be anything else, then his goodness is the product of an inner yearning, and not of an externally imposed compulsion. In other words he desires to be good, not because he is compelled to be by the fear of some external sanction, but because he wants to be with all the longing of his heart.

(b) But there is something even more far-reaching than that. No one can speak of conversion and speak no word of the great saving fact of justification by faith. God, in Paul's magnificent paradox, justifies the ungodly (Rom 4⁵). The verb is *dikaioun*. Greek verbs ending in *-oun* do not mean *to make* a man something; they mean *to treat or reckon or account* him as something. So then to say that God justifies the ungodly means quite simply that God in His amazing love treats the sinner as if he was a good man. Again to put it very simply, God loves us, not for anything that we are, but for what He is.

Now this has a paradoxical effect on a man's attitude to sin when he discovers this amazing truth. On the one hand, it makes sin more terrible than ever it was, for sin becomes a crime, not against law, but against love; it means not breaking God's law so much as breaking God's heart; and therefore it must leave us with an even greater horror at sin. But, on the other hand, if we may dare to put it so, it means that sin has ceased to matter, for not all our sin can cancel out the love of God. It puts us under the obligation to sweat blood and tears in the battle of goodness; but it also puts us in the position when in the moment of failure and falling we can still go back to God as a child who has been bad goes back to his mother.

It is true that the convert has laid upon him an obligation like no obligation in all the world because he has been loved with a love like no other love in the world; but the convert has also been given a peace like none in the world, for he knows that God loves him not for what he is but for what God is, and that therefore the eternal arms are ever open and the eternal heart is never shut to the man who has tried and who knows that he has fallen and failed.

We can only argue from the human to the divine, because we have no other language to use and no other thoughts to think. A son knows well that he must do nothing to grieve the heart of his parents; if he is in any sense a man of honour, he feels the binding obligation to be worthy of the love with which he has been surrounded since his birth. But he also knows that, if he makes shipwreck of things, even if every other door is shut against him, the door of his old home will still be open to him, and even if everyone else regards him as a criminal, his parents will still regard him as a son. That is exactly our relationship to God. The inescapable obligation demands the unremitting effort, but the immeasurable love brings the indestructible peace.

(iv) It may be said that there is only one place in Acts where, as it were, the obligations of the convert are laid down in black and white, and where there is anything like a rule and a regulation laid upon the convert. And the odd thing is that at first sight it is what we can only call a disappointing passage, although that reaction may well be qualified when we see the deeper and the fuller implications of it.

The passage in question occurs twice, in Acts 15[20, 29], and is the decision of the Council of Jerusalem regarding the obligations which must be laid upon Gentile converts who enter the Church. In Acts 15[19, 20] it runs as follows:

Therefore my judgement is that we should not trouble those of the Gentiles who turn to God, but should write to them to abstain from the pollutions of idols and from unchastity and from what is strangled and from blood.

In Acts 15[29] 'the pollutions of idols' becomes 'what has been sacrificed to idols', and thus it is made clear that the reference is to meat offered to idols, and that the rule is that Gentile converts must not ever eat meat which has been part of a heathen sacrifice.

The odd thing—and, as we have said, the at first sight disappointing thing—about this series of regulations is that three out of four of them deal with ritual and ceremonial laws and only one with an ethical matter. The convert is not to eat meat which has formed part of a heathen sacrifice. The Jew would never eat meat from which all the blood had not been drained, for the blood is the life and the blood belongs to God, for the life belongs to God (Gen 9[4]; Lev 7[26, 27], 17[10-14]; Deut 12[16, 23]). This automatically meant that a Jew could never eat the meat of an animal which had been strangled, because in that case the blood remains in the carcase; animals had to be slaughtered by having their throats cut, so that the blood would drain away. In point of fact, the abstention from blood and the abstention from things strangled say the same thing twice in slightly different ways.

The textual history of this passage makes it clear that this difficulty was felt. The various readings of this passage go in two directions.

(a) The Chester Beatty manuscript of Acts, P45,

certain manuscripts of the Ethiopic Version and possibly Origen omit 'from unchastity', and, if that phrase be omitted the regulation becomes completely ceremonial, with no ethical injunction at all.

(*b*) The Western Text, both in verses 20 and 29, omits 'from what is strangled', as do certain of the Vulgate manuscripts, and certain of the fathers, including Cyprian, Tertullian, Jerome, and Augustine. In all probability they then took 'the pollutions of idols' to mean idolatry in general and 'blood' to mean bloodshed—that is, murder. The same authorities, with the addition of certain minuscule manuscripts, and Irenaeus and Eusebius, then add at the end of the list of regulations the extra clause, 'and not to do to others anything that they do not wish done to themselves', which is, of course, the negative form of the Golden Rule. The result of this is that all the ritual and ceremonial material is removed, and the whole matter is ethicized into a series of rules for Christian conduct in which unchastity and violence are forbidden, and the Golden Rule in its negative form made the universal rule of life.

There is little doubt that the form of the regulations as given in the R.S.V. is correct, and that the other two forms are attempts to make the regulations, as it were, self-consistent in opposite directions.

As we have said, at first sight these regulations seem disappointing as a summary of the obligations to be laid on the convert to Christianity; but when we examine them more carefully, and when we understand the implications of them, we come to see that there is much more in them than that which lies upon the surface.

(i) They constitute a demand for uncompromising

65

purity. The Christian convert must abstain from all unchastity. It is the simple truth that Christianity brought into the world a new idea of sexual purity. The ancient world attached little stigma to sexual relationships either before marriage or outside marriage. They were indeed the customary and the accepted practice. In the period which is the immediate background of the New Testament, Seneca could say that there were Roman women who were married to be divorced and divorced to be married, and who distinguished the years, not by the names of the consuls, but by the names of their husbands (Seneca, *On Benefits*, 3.16.1-3). 'Innocence,' he says, 'is not rare; it is nonexistent' (*On Anger*, 2.8). Later Clement of Alexandria was to describe certain women as the personification of adultery, 'girt like Venus with a golden girdle of vice' (Clement of Alexandria, *Paedagogos*, 3.2-4). Juvenal tells how Messalina, the Empress wife of Claudius, used to slip out of the royal palace at nights and go down to serve in the common brothels. She was ever the last to leave, and would return to the imperial pillow with all the odours of the stews (Juvenal, *Satires*, 6.114-32).

As for homosexuality, it was what Döllinger called 'the great national disease of Greece' (*The Gentile and the Jew*, ii.239). J. J. Chapman says that it had become 'racial, indigenous, and ingrown like a loathsome fungus spreading steadily through a forest' (*Lucian, Plato and Greek Morals*, 132, 133). Into a world of sexual anarchy Christianity came with this new demand for absolute and uncompromising purity, insisting that a man must keep himself 'unstained from the world' (Jas 1[27]).

(ii) There is no difficulty in seeing the greatness of the moral demand on the convert; but it is the other two demands which seem to come from an altogether different sphere of life and thought. There is the demand to abstain from meat offered to idols. That this was no small problem is clear from the space which Paul devoted to the discussion of it (1 Cor 8). To the modern mind it does not seem to be a matter of much moment. But in New Testament times it involved an uncompromising break with paganism, an uncompromising witness for Christianity, and the almost certainly uncompromising farewell to the greater part of social life.

What happened was this. In the ancient world all great occasions had their ceremonial sacrifice; and this was as true of domestic life as it was of civic or national life. A wedding, a birthday, a time of thanksgiving would be celebrated with its appropriate sacrifice. Now on such occasions only a very small part of the animal was offered as a token sacrifice, sometimes no more than two or three hairs cut from the animal's forehead. Part of the meat was the perquisite of the Temple priests, but by far the greater part was given to the worshipper wherewith to make a sacrifice for his family and his friends, either in the temple itself or in his own house. The invitation to such a function actually ran: 'I invite you to dine with me at the table of the lord Serapis' (cp. *P. Oxy.*, 523; G. Milligan, *Selections from the Greek Papyri*, 97). A social occasion was essentially an act of worship. To such an occasion the convert was now forbidden to go. Meat offered to idols could never pass his lips, and he had therefore to say goodbye to friendship, to social fellowship, and maybe even to family

67

love. Herein—and it must have been hard to accept it—the Christian is summoned to make an act of uncompromising loyalty to Jesus Christ, even if it involved him in social loneliness and social ostracism. Here indeed the essential difference was clearly expressed.

(iii) The last injunction is in many ways the most interesting of all. As we have seen, it is purely a Jewish food law, and it enjoins the convert to abstain from anything that has been strangled and from blood. To the modern mind this seems a strange demand to set among the priorities in obligation which confront the convert. But in point of fact the significance of this goes very deep. The plain fact was that at that particular stage of the development of the Church table fellowship between Gentile and Jew would have been completely impossible without the observance of that regulation. It is quite true that in the end this also had to go, and the ceremonial law had to be completely abrogated. In the teaching of Jesus it was in principle abrogated. But at this stage it was still not possible for the Jew so completely to cease to be a Jew.

This, then, is the other side of the matter, and it was a sign that, although there are areas in which the Christian convert must be absolutely uncompromising, there are other areas in which compromise becomes a duty. And one area in which compromise on matters which are not matters of principle does become a duty is the area of Christian fellowship. In this particular instance the Gentile convert was being asked to accept the compromise of a deliberate self-limitation in order to preserve the unbroken fellowship of the Christian Church.

There is a time not to yield and there is a time to yield. In the matter of Christian purity, in the matter of Christian loyalty, compromise is impossible; but there are matters of the ordinary everyday affairs of life and in the conventions which govern them in which the same rigidity becomes not laudable, but blameworthy, for every man is under the obligation to self-denial and self-limitation in order to preserve Christian fellowship and Christian unity.

There is another passage in which Acts sets out the life of the convert, and, if the decisions which followed the Council of Jerusalem seem at first sight to be disappointing, this other passage seems much more near the permanent centre of the life of the Christian. It is the passage in Acts 2$^{42-7}$ which tells of the life of the first converts who were swept into the Church by the preaching of Peter. We quote it in full in the New English Bible translation:

They met constantly to hear the apostles teach, and to share the common life, to break bread, and to pray. A sense of awe was everywhere, and many marvels and signs were brought about through the apostles. All whose faith had drawn them together held everything in common; they would sell their property and their possessions and make a general distribution as the need of each required. With one mind they kept up their daily attendance at the temple, and, breaking bread in private houses, shared their meals with unaffected joy, as they praised God and enjoyed the favour of the whole people.

There stands the description of the life of the Christian convert. Let us analyse it to see the elements which were in it.

(i) They met constantly to hear the apostles teach.

That is to say, they devoted themselves to learning more and more about the faith into which they had entered. Here we come upon something which never should be forgotten. Conversion is a decisive event, but none the less conversion is only a beginning. It is the entry upon a journey, not the end of the road. It is the engagement upon a pilgrimage, not the arrival at the goal.

Let us take an analogy. Suppose that there is a locomotive which has to pull a train from London to Glasgow, and suppose that it is facing in the wrong direction. They will take it to the turn-table and they will turn it round; but after that it still has its 450-mile journey to go before it reaches the destination for which it is intended. Conversion is like the turning on the turn-table. In that moment and that decision a man reverses the direction of his life, but there still lie before him the long daily pilgrimage to God and the long daily growth in knowledge and in grace. The word for *sanctification* is *hagiasmos*; all Greek nouns which end in -*asmos* describe a process; and *hagiasmos* means the *road to holiness*. In the moment of conversion a man is justified; he knows that by the mercy of God he is in a new relationship with God; but he has still to be sanctified. And there are few things which have damaged the conception of the Christian life more than the idea that conversion is the end of the road. It may be the end of one road, but it is the beginning of another. The word *disciple* (*mathētēs*) literally means a *learner*, and the Christian must remain a learner to the end of the day.

(ii) They met to share the common life—that is to say, the convert enters into a fellowship. There is always a danger of making conversion an individualistic thing, in which a man is concerned only with the saving of his own soul. It may well be said that conversion is the end of individualism and the entry into fellowship.

It sometimes happens that a so-called conversion experience separates a man from his fellow-men, either by giving him a sense of spiritual superiority or by attaching him to some narrow and exclusive group. The measure of the reality of any man's conversion is the extent to which it unites him to his fellow-men as well as to God. As the older and the wiser Christian said to John Wesley when Wesley was contemplating living the life of a solitary: 'God knows nothing of solitary religion.' And, as Wesley himself somewhere said: 'No man ever went to heaven alone.'

Conversion is not only conversion towards a certain kind of life; it is conversion into a fellowship. And that is precisely where the Church comes into the picture. The convert becomes a child of God and a member of God's family, which is the Church.

It is a very significant fact that the pictures which describe the Christian life are so often what we might call 'group' pictures. There is the metaphor of the sheep and the flock (Jn 10$^{14-16}$); of the body and its members (1 Cor 12$^{12-27}$); of the house and the stones of which it is built (1 Pet 2^5; Eph 2$^{21,\ 22}$); of the household and the family and the members of it (1 Tim 3^{15}). Conversion means entry into a life of togetherness, both with God and with man.

(iii) Our passage goes on to show that this togetherness of the converted life is exemplified in four different directions:

(a) It is exemplified by *eating together*. Twice in this passage the phrase *breaking bread* occurs. Just what

71

this phrase means in Acts is something of a problem. Including the two instances in this present passage, the phrase occurs five times in Acts; and, when the different occurrences are taken individually, the phrase is susceptible of different meanings. To modern ears it has a certain sacramental sound. That meaning is borne out by Acts 20[7, 11]. Acts 20[7] speaks of Paul preaching in Troas on the first day of the week, when the disciples came together to break bread. In the same passage in Acts 20[11] it is used of a meal which Paul took with the Church in the evening. It is again used in Acts 27[33-6]. In this passage which is part of the story of the storm at sea, it is told how Paul urged the hard-pressed company to eat some food. It then goes on to say that Paul took bread, and when he had given thanks for it, he broke it and began to eat, whereat the others joined him in the meal. It is difficult to attach a narrowly sacramental meaning to the phrase in that case. In our present passage in verse 42 it occurs as it were without comment, but in verse 46 it is something which is done at home, and which, it seems, is equivalent to sharing a meal.

It is probably true that there are two things to be said here. First, it is highly unlikely that the sacrament had at this very early time been formalized into the merely symbolic meal which it is today. At this time the *Agapē*, the weekly Love Feast, a real meal in which all shared, was one of the great meetings of the Christian communities. The Church did actually meet to eat together. Second, it must have been true to say that then, as it should be but so seldom is now, every meal was a sacrament, that the very sight of a loaf of bread and a cup of wine brought men's thoughts back to the

72

love of God in Jesus Christ. And to this a third, and by no means irrelevant, fact may be added. The day of vast congregations had not yet come; the time when Christians were strangers to each other had not yet emerged. We are here still at the stage when the Church consisted of little groups meeting in each other's houses, and very closely linked to one another.

We are at a time—and the tragedy is that it is gone—when the convert entered a fellowship in which people were so close to one another that they shared together, not only the worship of the Church, but the fellowship of their homes, and when they were so close to Jesus Christ that each common meal became a meal at which He was host and they were guests, and in which every loaf of bread reminded them of His broken body. The convert entered into a life at which the dinner table was the Lord's Table as really as the communion table in any Church.

(b) It is exemplified by *praying together*. There are perhaps not so many actual direct references to prayer in Acts as one might expect to find; but they follow a clear and most significant pattern.

First, prayer was habitual. A Jew, if he was devout, always prayed at the third, the sixth, and the ninth hours, at 9 a.m., at 12 midday, and at 3 p.m. So we find that Peter was praying at the sixth hour, as any devout Jew would be doing (Acts 10⁹). The convert entered into a life in which prayer was part of the essential pattern of life.

Second, we find that prayer is always the prelude to decision. The disciples prayed before they proceeded to the choice of one to replace the traitor Judas in the apostolic band (Acts 1²⁴, ²⁵); before the setting apart of the chosen Seven (Acts 6^6); for the coming of the Holy Spirit on the converts newly entered into the Church in Samaria (Acts 8^{15}); before the commissioning of Saul and Barnabas for the epoch-making first missionary journey (Acts 13^3); and Peter was at prayer before the arrival of the emissaries of Cornelius which was the prelude to the acceptance of the Gentiles (Acts 10^9). The convert entered into a life in which every step was dictated and directed by the deliberately sought guidance of God.

Third, we find that every crisis in life is met with prayer. The arrest of Peter and John, with all its perilous possibilities, is met with prayer (Acts 4$^{24-30}$); Stephen met death with prayer (Acts 7$^{59, 60}$); Peter faces the death of Dorcas with prayer (Acts 9^{40}); there is concentrated prayer for Peter when he was in prison (Acts 12^5).

One thing is notable in all these instances. In all of them the Christians did not so much ask things from God; rather they lifted the whole situation in which they were into the presence and the power of God. For the early Church prayer was not so much a series of definite requests, as it so often can become; prayer was rather an activity in which the human situation was lifted into the divine.

The convert entered into a life in which he did not so much request and even demand things from God, but in which he took everything in which he was involved and lifted it into God's presence. What the Christian wanted in these early days was not so much an answer from God as God Himself.

(c) It is exemplified by *the sharing of the common things of life*. They had everything in common, and they

74

sold their possession and put them into a common stock on which all members of the fellowship could draw as they had need. So Barnabas, who had an estate of his own, when he was converted to Christianity, sold it and laid the money at the apostles' feet (Acts 4[36, 37]).

The society into which the convert entered was a society in which fellowship was not simply a vague and sentimental general benevolence; fellowship was something which issued in practical and costly and sacrificial aid to those who were in need. James rounds on those who thought that fellowship could be adequately expressed in a kindly word and a pious wish: 'Suppose a brother or sister is in rags with not enough food for the day, and one of you says, "Good luck to you, keep yourself warm, and have plenty to eat", but does nothing to supply their bodily needs, what is the good of that?' (Jas 2[15, 16], N.E.B.). It is the teaching of Jesus that the reality of a man's conversion is to be tested by that man's reaction to the needs of those who are in want and trouble (Matt 25[31-46]). Conversion involves the acceptance of the obligation of the social gospel.

This needs to be said. There are those who speak with a vast and superior contempt of those whom they label 'do-gooders'. The New Testament thinks a very great deal of these same do-gooders. The verb *agathopoein*, to do good, occurs nine times in the New Testament, and four of these instances are on the lips of Jesus; four of the other instances are in 1 Peter, which was written at a time when Christianity was under fire, and when Peter saw the defence of Christianity precisely in this doing good. Peter also uses the noun *agathopoiia*, which means doing good, and the noun *agathopoios*, one

75

who does good (Mk 3[4]; Lk 6[9, 33, 35]; 1 Pet 2[14, 15, 20], 3[6, 17], 4[19]). 'The well-doer, the man who does the good and the kind thing, is a child of God' (3 Jn 11). 'It is God's will', says Peter, 'that by doing good you should put to silence the ignorance of foolish men' (1 Pet 2[15]). It is the plain teaching of the New Testament that the so often despised do-gooder ranks higher in the hierarchy of God than the cloistered saint absorbed in his prayers, or the theologian or the philosopher withdrawn in his thoughts and his books. As the anonymous poet had it:

On me nor Priest nor Presbyter nor Pope,
  Bishop nor Dean may stamp a party name;
But Jesus, with his largely human scope,
  The service of my human life may claim.
Let prideful priests do battle about creeds,
  The Church is mine that does most Christlike deeds.

Or as Leigh Hunt had it:

Abou Ben Adhem (may his tribe increase!)
Awoke one night from a deep dream of peace,
And saw, within the moonlight in his room,
Making it rich, and like a lily in bloom,
An angel writing in a book of gold:—
Exceeding peace had made Ben Adhem bold,
And to the presence in the room he said,
'What writest thou?'—The vision rais'd its head,
And with a look made of all sweet accord,
Answer'd, 'The names of those who love the Lord.'
'And is mine one?' said Abou. 'Nay, not so,'
Replied the angel. Abou spoke more low,
But cheerly still; and said, 'I pray thee, then,

> *Write me as one that loves his fellow men.'*
> *The angel wrote, and vanish'd. The next night*
> *It came again with a great wakening light,*
> *And show'd the names whom love of God had blessed,*
> *And lo! Ben Adhem's name led all the rest.*

No so-called convert to Christ is a real convert unless his conversion makes him care sacrificially for his fellow-men, and express that care in the most practical way.

(d) It was exemplified by *worshipping together*. They attended the Temple together daily. There are two dangerous tendencies in modern times. First, there is the claim that we can worship God anywhere and everywhere, and therefore that the attendance at the worship of the Church is by no means essential. It is perfectly true, as Morris Abel Beer wrote, that:

> *Who builds a church within his heart*
> *And takes it with him everywhere*
> *Is holier far than he whose Church*
> *Is but a one-day house of prayer.*

No one would wish to deny that the whole earth is the temple of God and that we can worship Him anywhere. But there is this also to be said. A very great deal of the excitement would go out of any football match if there was only one spectator; a very great thrill goes out of a symphony if it is listened to alone. That is precisely why radio and television can never wholly replace live performance. There is a thrill in doing things together, for men are meant to do things together. It is so with worship. To be one of a worshipping company of people is a privilege not lightly to be abandoned. As Coleridge had it:

77

O sweeter than the marriage-feast,
'Tis sweeter far to me,
To walk together to the kirk
With a goodly company!

To walk together to the kirk,
And all together pray,
While each to his great Father bends,
Old men, and babes, and loving friends,
And youths and maidens gay!

The truly converted man knows the joy of worshipping together, and knows that there is no substitute for it.

The second thing is even more serious. There is a certain type of conversion which leaves a man critical, and often harshly critical, of the Church, and which often leads him into a smaller and smaller sect, in which he thinks he will find a special piety and a better holiness. No man will be blind to the faults of the Church, for the Church is a human as well as a divine institution, but the truly converted man will know the truth of Tertullian's saying that a man cannot have God for his Father unless he has the Church for his mother; and the truly converted man will have the humility to know that he too is far from perfect, and his conversion will unite him to men rather than separate him from them.

There is something wrong with a conversion which does not bring the sense of joy in worshipping together.

(iv) There are certain other things in this passage still to be gathered up, certain other characteristics of the life into which the converted man enters.

(a) It is a *power-conscious* life. 'Fear came upon every soul; and many wonders and signs were done by the apostles.' It is an eventful life, because it is always conscious of God in action. In the Christless life nothing seems to happen; in the Christ-filled life there are evidences everywhere that God is in action. It is the life, not conscious of some distant past in which God once acted mightily, but certain that the arm of God is not shortened and the power of God not grown less. It is the life not only of memory, but also of hope, the life not only of recollection, but also of expectation.

(b) It is *a joyous, a generous, and a grateful* life. They partook of their food with glad and generous hearts, praising God. The converted man is the happy man. When Collie Knox was in the Army, religion became real to him, and the main consequence of it at the time was that he was distressed and worried. E. S. Woods was at the time the chaplain of the regiment, and Woods said to him: 'Young Knox, don't make an agony of your religion.' It was said of Robert Burns that he was 'haunted rather than helped' by his religion. The great Christians have been characteristically happy. Take, for instance, two men poles apart, yet both marked by this overflowing joy. There was St Francis of Assisi, the troubadour of Christ, singing his way through life, and there was D. L. Moody, of whom a journalist who was attached to one of his missions and who travelled with him said: 'The trouble about Mr Moody is that he is so often so unbearably funny.' The converted man knows well that he is a sinner, but he knows the far greater truth that he is a forgiven sinner, and, as the old hymn has it, there is sunshine in his heart today. Dr R. W. Dale said of D. L. Moody: 'He preached in a manner that produced the effect produced by Luther, and provoked similar criticism.

He exulted in the free grace of God. . . . His joy was contagious. Men leaped out of darkness into light.'

The converted man is the generous man. Freely he has received, freely he must give (Matt 10⁸). The heart of God is in him, and the heart of God is a generous heart.

The converted man is the grateful man. He is above all conscious of the great things God has done for him, and there is room for nothing but gratitude in his heart.

(*c*) Last of all, it is a *lovely* life. The Christians had favour with all the people. Quite simply, that means that everybody liked them.

One of the most significant things of all is the word which the New Testament repeatedly uses for *good*. It is the word *kalos*, and *kalos* describes something which is not merely good in the moral sense of the term, but something which is winsome and attractive and lovely to see. When the Pastoral Epistles were written, Christianity was a little island in a sea of surrounding paganism, and in such circumstances the personal, daily life of the Christian was of supreme importance, and in these letters this word *kalos* occurs no fewer than eighteen times. To take but one example, the Christian is to be rich in good deeds (1 Tim 6¹⁸). The word for good is *kalos*; the Christian life is to be rich in lovely things.

The life of the Christian convert must acquire a sheen of loveliness. J. P. Struthers—and how well he followed his own advice—used to say that what would aid the cause of Christ more than anything else would be if Christians far oftener than they do were to do a 'bonnie thing'. The converted man must convert others by the sheer radiant, winsome, attractive grace of his life. It is not without its significance that the word *charis* means *grace*, but it also means *charm*. The dreary, unattractive, dullness of so much alleged Christian living stands exposed and condemned.

E

Chapter VI

The Obligations of the Church

WE have thought about the obligations of the convert; but there is another side to this. There are the obligations of the Church to the convert. This is something which the Church has too often taken far too lightly. When a child is baptized, the ceremony of baptism ends with the intimation that this child is now one with us in the Lord. When people are received into full membership of the Church, they are welcomed, often with the right hand of fellowship, into the household and the family of the faith. Far too often that is the end of the matter. The whole responsibility for the newly received child or member is left with the minister of the Church. But the obligation to the convert is no an obligation which is laid solely on the minister; it is laid on the congregation. The Church is as responsible for the new convert as the parent is for the child; and, if the Church neglects that responsibility, the Church is just as culpable as the parent who neglects the parental obligation within the sphere of the home. Too often there is far too little effort to maintain a living contact with the new entrant into the Christian faith and Church.

(i) There is the obligation of *teaching* the convert. It is very significant how often the word teaching enters into the activities of the Church in the story of Acts.

The disciples were teaching the people with a vigour and an effectiveness which aroused the opposing anger of the orthodox Jewish leaders (Acts 4^2, 5^{25}). Paul and Barnabas were teaching and preaching the word of the Lord (Acts 15^{35}). For a whole year Paul and Barnabas were teaching the people in Antioch (Acts 11^{26}). In Ephesus both in public and from house to house Paul spent his time teaching the people (Acts 20^{20}); and even in his last imprisonment in Jerusalem he had not abandoned his teaching ministry (Acts 28^{31}).

The failure of many an evangelistic campaign to produce lasting effects is due precisely to the fact that the presentation of the grace of God and the demand for decision were not followed by an equally deliberate teaching campaign of educational evangelism.

One of the notable characteristics of the great evangelists is the study which they undertook themselves, and which they provided for their converts. A Chicago minister said of D. L. Moody: 'One day I found him in his room trying to get up a sermon. He had thrown off his coat and was struggling with his Bible and a concordance while the sweat ran down his face.' During the Baltimore campaign Mrs Moody wrote to a friend: 'Mr Moody has made quite a *rigid* rule whereby he takes six hours each day for study.' During the American Civil War a soldier was touched by the preaching of Moody. He said: 'The next morning, or soon after, I went to my dog tent, opened a little copy of the New Testament which some men of the Christian Commission had given to me, and then and there began to read and pray my way into the Kingdom of Christ.' The way in was by reading and by prayer.

We may take the analogy of a lad choosing the trade,

83

the vocation, or the profession which he will follow. He makes his choice; he turns his face in the direction which he wishes his life to take. But he will certainly never arrive at that goal without the study and the labour and the toil and the thought which are the price of achievement. Just so with the convert. He makes his decision, but he has still to find out what he believes, why he believes it, and how he can communicate it.

Real conversion cannot mean other than the dedication of the total self to Jesus Christ. Part of that total self is the mind, and, as J. S. Whale has said, it is a moral duty to be intelligent. That is not to say that we can reduce Christianity to a neat series of propositions and proofs; but not to try to understand is to commit intellectual suicide. Long ago Plato said that the unexamined life is the life not worth living, and the unexamined faith is the faith not worth having. Unless a faith is tested and possessed, unless belief becomes conviction, unless decision is based on something more than a moment of emotion, then faith will not stand against the assaults of life, but will quite inevitably collapse.

It is further true that the convert will now go out into a world which is sometimes indifferent to, sometimes hostile to, sometimes even resentful of Christianity. He will go out into a world where there are such things as Communism which are not so much rival political creeds as they are rival religions. He will go out into a situation which has perhaps never existed before. Hitherto, people have almost universally accepted the Christian ethic, if they did not accept the Christian theology. They have agreed that the Christian way of life is right. But now there has arisen a situation in which even the Christian ethic is violently under fire. And to send a convert out into a situation like that without an intelligent grip and grasp of the Christian faith is equivalent to sending him into battle naked and unarmed. Nothing is today more necessary than that the Church should remember its teaching obligation to the converts who have entered its fellowship.

(ii) There is the obligation of *strengthening* the convert. Paul went from place to place through the region of Galatia and Phrygia, strengthening all the disciples (Acts 18²³). He commends the elders of Ephesus to the word of God's grace which is able to build them up (Acts 20³²). The implication is that the Christian life is a growth and an upbuilding, and for that growth and upbuilding the Church is responsible.

And yet in spite of this fact there is so much of what we might well call static Christianity; there are even people who take a pride in the fact that they have never moved from the position in which they began. There is a grim law of life that there can be no such thing as standing still; there is either development or death, movement or paralysis. The Church is responsible for producing in those who enter it a deepening grasp of the faith, a daily movement closer to God, a growing grace of character, and increasing victory over temptation, a daily growth into the likeness of Jesus Christ. It may be that one of the greatest condemnations of the Church is its satisfaction with static Christianity.

(iii) There is the obligation of *admonishing* the convert. It is Paul's claim that in Ephesus for three years he did not cease night or day to admonish everyone with tears (Acts 20³¹). It is the Church's duty to give to the

85

convert advice, guidance, and rebuke where it is necessary.

It is one of the features of the modern Church that it has abdicated from its responsibility for discipline. No one will deny that there have been times when discipline was applied in the Church in a censorious, self-righteous and completely unsympathetic spirit; but there is a world of difference between that and the refusal to exert discipline at all. We have only to read the New Testament to see a situation in which no threatening situation was allowed to develop unchecked and no unchristian conduct left without its rebuke administered in love.

It is a tragic characteristic of the modern Church that it is dully and resignedly accepted that a man's acceptance of membership of the Church need make very little difference in his life.

(iv) There is the obligation of *encouraging* the convert. We read of Paul going through the regions of Macedonia and giving the Christians there much encouragement (Acts 20²). J. C. Pollock, in his biography of D. L. Moody, tells of a small boy who every Sunday walked three miles to Moody's Sunday school, although there was a Sunday school near his own home. When asked why he was prepared to make this journey to Moody's school each week, his answer was: 'They love a fellow over there.' If there is one thing that the Christian fellowship ought to do, it is that it should surround the entrant into it with a warmth of love. The Church nowadays, with its many members and its organization, has at least in some cases become almost completely impersonal—and an impersonal Church is a contradiction in terms. It is too often true that the 'official' Church looks askance at the new enthusiasms and the adventurous spirit of the new convert. He who enters the Church has a right to look for encouragement in the Christian way, whether that encouragement be needed in a time of new adventure or in a time of shame and failure.

The Church needs the convert; from the Church the convert should receive the teaching, the strengthening, the admonishing, the encouraging which will help him to walk in the Christian way.

Chapter VII

Conversion Today

WE must finally look at the idea of conversion in
the modern situation in which we find ourselves
today.

(i) Of the reality of the phenomenon of conversion
there can never be any doubt. That people have been
and are converted is a fact which does not admit of
denial. At the close of D. L. Moody's New York
campaign the *New York Times*, which had been at first
completely hostile to him, wrote: 'The work accomplished this winter by Mr Moody in this city for private
and public morals will live. The drunken have become
sober, the vicious virtuous, the worldly and self-seeking
unselfish, the ignoble noble, the impure pure, the youth
have started with more generous aims, the old have
stirred from grossness. A new hope has lifted up
hundreds of human beings, a new consolation has come
to the sorrowful, and a better principle has entered the
sordid life of the day through the labours of these plain
men.' During the Boston campaign the (Boston)
Sunday Times, very far from being a religious paper and
not altogether agreeing with what was happening
wrote: 'The masses in Boston are undoubtedly becoming permeated with piety.' R. W. Dale of Birmingham,
a man in almost every way poles apart from D. L.
Moody, said of those who came to the after-meetings in

Birmingham: 'They had come up into the gallery anxious, restless, feeling after God in the darkness', and after a conversation of fifteen or twenty minutes 'their faces were filled with joy, and they left me not only at peace with God but filled with joy. . . . These people carried their new joy with them to their houses and their workshops. It could not be hid.' Of Moody's East End campaign in London, J. C. Pollock writes that among the results was that dockers swore less and duchesses were no longer afraid openly to speak about God. Dockers and duchesses alike were touched with this new power.

Of the reality of this fact of conversion there is no doubt; but it is doubtful if even the greatest twentieth-century evangelical campaigns had quite the same effect that the nineteenth-century ones had. Somehow there has been a change.

(ii) There is still less doubt regarding the need of the present situation for this converting power.

There is need within the Church. We have already seen that in the New Testament the Christians are the *hagioi*, the saints; and we have seen that the basic idea of this is that the Christian is *different* from the world; in point of fact, the Church has undergone a process of continual adjustment to the world and an increasing conformity to the world, until the lines of demarcation are obscured and it is by no means always clear who is the Christian and who is the man of the world. The number of pledged, committed, decisive Christians is perilously small.

There is need within society in general. The moral tone of society is shockingly low; the sanctity of the marriage bond is undermined; the unnatural vices flourish; the menace of drugs has become more acute than it ever was before in this country; crimes of violence increase. And what is to be said of a society in which the educational authorities think it necessary to set up special classes in certain schools for schoolgirls who are unmarried mothers? The need for a turning to God is self-evident. Even the non-Christian will be moved to alarm at the realization that we have come to a stage when not only Christian theology but even the Christian ethic is under deliberate attack.

(iii) But there are difficulties involved, and these difficulties must be fairly and squarely faced.

(a) We cannot, even if we wanted to do so, reproduce the situation of the early Church. We cannot reproduce the situation in which a man was lifted out of one religion into another. Nor can we reproduce a situation in which men were hearing the name of Jesus Christ and the offers and demands of the Christian religion as something absolutely new. Whatever we may say about our present situation, it remains deeply permeated with the Christian ideal and the Christian way of belief. Men know what the Christian ethic is; men know at least something of Jesus Christ and what He was like. We cannot reproduce the situation of a man who had never heard the name of Jesus Christ, who had never heard the demand of the Christian life, who had worshipped some other god or goddess all his days, or at least we cannot reproduce it outside the mission field. The basic difference today is that we are not asking a man to accept something absolutely new and something of which he has never even heard before; we are rather asking him to submit to something which in some sense he has always known. The approach cannot be the same. Christianity is no longer a little island in a sea of paganism, under deliberate and savage attack, or at least ever open to the possibility of such attack. Christianity is in fact the conventionally accepted national religion. A man today may be asked to step out of indifference or even hostility into Christianity; he cannot be asked to step out of entire ignorance of it.

J. C. Pollock tells of an incident when Moody was working as a chaplain among the soldiers in the American Civil War. 'Chaplain,' said a dying soldier to him, 'help me to die. I've been fighting Christ all my life. I had a praying mother and I disregarded her prayers always.' The state of that man is not the state of a man who is confronted with the offer of something previously unheard of; it is the state of a man who is called upon to face something which he had always known was there and which he had hitherto chosen to disregard. And that is the typical situation at least in what is known as Western civilization today.

(*b*) It is no small problem that the whole idea of conversion, even the very word *conversion*, tends to be associated with a certain kind and type of religion, that type of religion which is known as 'evangelical'. It in fact often seems as if only that type of religion was interested in conversion at all. There can be a certain suspicion and tension between those who, so to speak, make conversion the one aim of religion, and those who almost shrink away from the word altogether. This is a very wrong situation, for surely it must be the aim of all religion to persuade a man to turn to God—and that is precisely what conversion is. Not to put too fine a point upon it, the situation has come very near to being one in which one side regards conversion as belonging to the manifestations of the lower forms of religion which are almost distasteful to an intellectual, while the other side regards failure to deal in decision as almost ruling a man out of religion altogether.

(*c*) Perhaps the most serious mistake of all has been the tendency to standardize the experience of conversion, and to take as the norm the experience of Paul on the Damascus Road. The inevitable result of this has been the implication that the normal conversion experience must be sudden, shattering, and complete.

It would not take a great deal of thought to show the unsatisfactory and indeed untenable nature of any such view. It is by no means irrelevant to remember that there is a very real sense in which Paul's conversion was anything but sudden. It is quite clear from the whole nature of the narrative that for long Paul had been kicking against the pricks, for long he had been battling against the fascination of Jesus Christ, for long he had been resisting the pull of the love of God. The very violence of his activity against Christ shows the intensity of his effort to silence the fascination. In the case of Paul certainly the break was sudden, but the break was simply the sudden surrender of a man who could fight no longer. But there is something far more significant than that. Paul was a man who was deliberately out to obliterate Jesus Christ; he was on his way to murder as many Christians as he could find; he was breathing out threatenings and slaughter; he was out to devastate the Church and to leave it as an army leaves a scorched earth and sacks a city. The very word he uses of his activity (*porthein*; Gal 1[13]) is the word that is normally used for an army sacking a city.

Now it is clear that the number of men and women in whom that situation is reproduced is infinitesimal. Indifference may have to be broken through; the unawareness of sin may have to be replaced by the searing consciousness of sin; hostility may have to surrender; but this murderous passion of hatred and persecution can hardly at all be paralleled. In other words, the ordinary person cannot have the Pauline experience; and to make that experience the standard for conversion is to make the exception the rule. If it is true that there are as many ways to the stars as there are men to climb them, if it is true that God has His own secret stairway into every heart, if it is true that God fulfils Himself in many ways, then clearly there will be no one standardized conversion experience; but the experience of conversion will be as infinitely varied as human experience itself. Nevertheless, certain things can be said.

1. No one will deny that the sudden experience can and does blessedly happen. When A. C. Benson heard Moody preach at Cambridge at the end of the service, he tells us, he went out 'into the night like one dizzied with a sudden blow'. Of course, it is blessedly true that the sinner can become the saint with an experience like a lightning flash, and the Christ who was on the circumference of life can suddenly be in the middle of life with an explosive suddenness.

2. But there are other ways to conversion. Take the case of a child who from his earliest days has known the name of Jesus, a child whose first intelligent words were a good-night prayer, and whose first experience of literature was the Shepherd Psalm. There can be no necessity for a sudden change there, for that child has

never faced in any direction but in the direction of God. Someone asked Thoreau: 'Have you made your peace with God?' His answer was: 'I never knew He was my enemy.' There can have been few preachers with the converting power of Phillips Brooks, yet once when Dr Vinton spoke to Brooks, when he was a young man, about being converted, Brooks said that he did not know what conversion meant. He had no moment of identifiable crisis in his spiritual life (W. R. Bowie, *Men of Fire*, p. 181). There are people for whom Christian experience is not an explosion but a growth, for there was no time in life when they did not know and love their Lord.

3. But there is certainly this to be said. The person who has had this growing and developing experience of the Lord he has always known may well need to be reminded that there are others who do need the radical change. F. B. Meyer discovered this through the work of D. L. Moody in York. He was a very young minister then. He said of that mission in York: 'For me it was the birthday of new conceptions of ministry, new methods of work, new inspirations and hopes. . . . I had been brought up in a holy home. I had been in business for a little, then took my degree at College, but I didn't know anything about conversion, or about the gathering of sinners around Christ, and I owe everything, everything in my life, I think, to that parlour room where the first time I found people broken hearted about sin. I learned the psychology of the soul. I learned how to point men to God.' The man who has never been away from God has to learn that there are those who have journeyed in the far countries of the soul.

4. But now one all-important thing must be said. We

have said that there is no standard conversion experience; we have said that one man may accept Jesus Christ as Lord in one shattering moment, and that for another there may be an uninterrupted process and development. But in the difference there remains one common factor—there must in every life be some moment of decision.

In the one case it will be a moment in which the direction of life is even violently reversed, in which a man breaks with the old way and accepts the new. In the second case the decision will be a decision regarding the Church. It will be a moment of choice when a man decides to accept all the responsibilities, when he has for so long enjoyed the privileges; it will be a moment when he publicly and spontaneously proclaims his loyalty to Jesus Christ; it will be a moment when he deliberately takes his stand beside the Christ whom he has known for long. It is not so much the acceptance of something new as it is the public and definite affirmation of something which has for long existed.

Here then comes the crux of the matter. In the one case it is the acceptance of Christ; in the other case it is deliberate, self-chosen entry into the Church. For very many the moment of decision will be the moment of the acceptance of full membership of the Church which is the Body of Jesus Christ. If that be so, the moment of entry into Church membership should be the most decisive moment in a man's life. It should be an act of the most definite and far-reaching decision. 'All Christian apologetic', Dr Soper rightly says, 'breaks down unless it prompts those who speak and those who hear to a decision about Jesus Christ.'

There follows one inevitable conclusion. In far too many cases as things are today entry into Church membership is far too easy, for too undemanding, and far too indecisive. Too often the training for it is inadequate and the method of it unimpressive. There is too much opportunity to drift or slip into the Church, and too little opportunity to mark entry into the Church as the great decisive moment in a man's life. It is more than worth while to contrast the modern way of entry into the Church with that which obtained in the early days.

There were two very different stages in the Church's methods with those who were moved to seek entry into its membership.

The first stage is the stage pictured within the New Testament itself. At that stage baptism immediately followed conversion. The Ethiopian eunuch (Acts 8^{36-8}) and the Philippian gaoler (Acts 16^{30-4}) were baptized as soon as they believed. The Apostolic preaching demanded, and resulted in, immediate baptism. But even at this stage there is something which has to be added to this. The teachers at that stage are always marked out as foundation pillars of the organization of the Church. They ranked with the apostles and the prophets (1 Cor 12^{28}; cp. Eph 4^{12}; Acts 13^1). Quite obviously, the Church regarded teaching as one of its main functions. Therefore, even at that early stage there was more to membership of the Church than immediate entry. Teaching was an essential part of the reception of its new members, but it does seem that the teaching came after rather than before baptism.

In the second stage the Church had come to a situation in which it knew that for the welfare of the Church membership of the Church must be made possible for the genuine believer, but impossible for the person whose belief was merely a superficial reaction. Before we speak of what happened in detail we may set out the broad pattern of it. A man came to the Church; he was tested; he was instructed; he was tested again; he was baptized; he entered the Church, and then he was very much under the discipline of the Church. This stage is fully described in the *Apostolic Tradition* of Hippolytus, which describes the situation round about A.D. 200. When a man came asking to be allowed into the Church first of all, his motives were thoroughly examined, and his sponsors had to affirm his fitness to receive instruction. His family life was examined to see that he was living in moral purity. If he was a slave, and if his master was already a Christian, his master had to testify that he was an honest and good servant. There is a long list of trades and professions and activities which, if he was engaged in them, he had to abandon before he was accepted even for instruction. A man would not be accepted even as a possible candidate for Church membership if he was a pander, a sculptor or painter engaged in the making of heathen idols, an actor, a pantomimist, a teacher (who inevitably had to observe the state religion), a charioteer, a gladiator, if he was an official or performer in any of the gladiatorial shows, a heathen priest, a tender of idols, a soldier, a military commander, a civil magistrate, a harlot, sodomite, a self-castrated person, a magician, an enchanter, an astrologer, a diviner, a soothsayer, a user of magic verses, a juggler, a mountebank, an amulet-maker (*The Apostolic Tradition*, 16).

Even the admission to the state of catechumen was a

97

solemn process involving prayer, the laying on of hands and the sign of the Cross. The period of instruction lasted for no less than three years (*The Apostolic Tradition*, 17). There were ordinarily four stages in the catechumenate. First, a man was under private instruction, and was not yet fully received. Second, he became a *hearer*, during which time he was allowed to hear Scripture read and the sermon preached by the bishop, but was not allowed into the prayer part of the service—not even to the prayer for catechumens proper. Third, he became a *kneeler*, during which stage he was allowed to remain for the prayers. Third, he became one of the *competentes* or *electi*, at which stage he was an immediate candidate for baptism and had been examined and approved by the bishop.

There followed another testing of him. The lives of the catechumens were examined to see whether 'they have lived soberly, whether they have honoured the widows, whether they have visited the sick, whether they have been active in well-doing' (*The Apostolic Tradition*, 20). Only when they had passed all these stages were they finally accepted for baptism, which was itself a ceremony which no one was likely to forget. Before all this, the catechumen, of course, could not share in the Eucharist, nor even in the prayers of the faithful.

Once in the Church the Church member was very much under control of the Church. The Canons of the various Councils again and again clearly lay down the penance which must be done by Church members who are guilty of various sins. A Church member who lapsed must undergo penance for from anything from two to thirteen years (Canons of Nicaea 11, 12, 14).

An adulterer or adulteress had to do seven years' penance, a woman who used drugs to procure abortion ten years', a wilful murderer penance for life, an involuntary homicide five years', diviners, sorcerers, and astrologers five years', one who was guilty of seduction ten years' (Canons of Ancyra, 22-5). Prayers for those under penance followed the prayers for the catechumens, and those under penance had to leave before the prayers for the faithful and, of course, before the Eucharist.

We have cited this evidence to show how decisive a step the acceptance of Church membership was. It is not suggested that this ancient pattern should still be followed, but it is suggested that in the modern situation the act of decision in becoming a member of the Church should be very much more definite than it is, and that the demand of Church membership should be very much more binding than it is.

The necessity of decision is paramount. There are two kinds of decision. There is the decision of the man who has been a stranger to Christ and the faith; but there is the equally important decision of the man who has always been within the Christian faith, but for whom the act of deliberate acceptance must be equally decisive.

(iv) We have seen both the reality and necessity of conversion, and we have seen the difficulties which are involved. It remains finally to look at the particular approach to conversion which is necessary today.

(a) The approach to conversion must be much less one-sided than it often has been. It must think much more in terms of the total man. It must think in terms of a man's intellect as well as in terms of a man's heart. Rightly or wrongly, the idea of conversion has become attached to a certain kind of mass meeting, a certain kind of hymn and music, a certain kind of theology. Rightly or wrongly, the ideas of conversion and of scholarship have become divorced. It has often been the case that those who were most concerned with conversion have regarded theological colleges as dangerous places, and have even tried to protect their people against the infection which emanates from such places and from those who teach in them.

It is perfectly true that Moody's question to George Adam Smith is entirely justified: 'Why talk of two Isaiahs when most people don't know of one?' But this is not the kind of thing of which we are thinking. We are thinking of a religion which refuses to look the results of modern science in the face, and which still regards the Bible as a scientific textbook. We are thinking of an approach which deals always in a vocabulary which has become completely conventional and completely undefined. Take a simple sentence: Believe on the Lord Jesus Christ and you will be saved. That sentence involves at least three questions: What do you mean by *believe*? Who is this Jesus? What do you mean by *saved*? Donald Soper has said that his vast experience of answering the questions of ordinary people leads him to believe that there are only three fundamental questions in which everyone is interested: Where have I come from? Where am I going? How am I to get there? All of these questions have to be faced by the mind as well as by the heart.

The result of thinking along these lines is startling. The result is that there is today a need for educational evangelism such as has never before existed. Now, if one thing is certain, it is that educational evangelism cannot be carried out by the mass meeting, so-called revivalistic technique. That technique can quite certainly arouse interest; it can quite certainly stab people awake. But once the interest has been aroused, once the mind and the heart have been awakened, the process of education and of thought can only take place within the Church. This is the kind of process which no itinerant evangelist can carry out, for the very simple reason that he is itinerant.

The necessity today is quite simple. It is that the Church should rediscover that conversion is its business, and should not be content to leave conversion to the special mission and the special evangelist, and that the Church should rediscover that her finest instrument towards conversion is teaching, teaching with such honesty, with such cogency, with such relevance, and with such evangelical devotion that the hearer is first interested, then convinced, and finally moved to decision. To produce real conversion the Church must unite teaching and decision, so that a man's heart and mind combine to leave him no alternative to accepting Jesus Christ as Lord.

(b) Secondly, the approach to conversion must be much less individualistic than it has so often been. Conversion has so often seemed to be concerned simply with man as an individual and with the saving of the man's own individual soul. There are three reasons why a man must be converted. Certainly, he must be converted for his own sake. Also, he must be converted for God's sake. But there is a real sense in which he must be converted for the sake of the community of which he is a part. Quite certainly, conversion must be concerned with a man not only as an individual but as a member of a community. Donald Soper, speaking of the crowd whose questions he has sought to answer for so many years, says: 'It has no time for a religion which confines itself to the work of converting individuals and has nothing authoritative to say about war or unemployment.' Sangster once set down a list of the things which revival would do for Britain:

1. It would pay old debts.
2. It would reduce sexual immorality.
3. It would disinfect the theatre.
4. It would cut the divorce rate.
5. It would reduce juvenile crime.
6. It would lessen the prison population.
7. It would improve the quality and increase the output of work.
8. It would restore to the nation a high sense of destiny.
9. It would make us invincible in the war of ideas.
10. It would give happiness and peace to the people.

It may well be that the greatest inadequacy in the older approach to conversion was simply its essential selfishness, the fact that it appeared to be mainly concerned to save the individual man from hell and to ensure the arrival of the individual man in heaven. An individual gospel without a social gospel is a sadly truncated thing. Conversion today must aim to make Christians who are not only concerned with their own souls but who are also acutely aware of their responsibilities to their fellow-men.

(c) Every step of this argument has been converging on one point. There ought to be a much closer connexion between conversion and the Church. It is the strange and odd fact that as things now are it is not in the Church that we expect to find conversions happening. We have actually come to a state of things when we expect to find conversions happening at missions and campaigns outside the Church rather than within the ordinary work, ministry, and activity of the Church. We ought to strive for a situation in which every entry into the membership of the Church is the product of a perfectly definite act of decision, the prelude to a comprehensive course of instruction, the self-dedication towards being the leaven which works in the community until the community becomes the Kingdom of God. Conversion will never be what it was meant to be until it happens within the Church, and the Church will never be what it was meant to be until each man who enters it, enters it in conscious and deliberate decision. This is far from meaning that everyone who comes to the Church and its services and its activities will have made that decision, but it does mean that the ultimate end and aim of all the coming must be decision for Christ, instruction in the Christian faith, and dedication to the service of the men and the world for whom the King and the Head of the Church once died.

Chapter VIII

Epilogue: The Christian Way

IT is a great joy to know that you have decided to set out upon the Christian Way. It is very natural that you should be asking, 'Just what does it mean to be a Christian? What difference should it make in my life? What is going to be the practical effect of being a Christian on my daily life and living?'

Do you remember the invitation that Jesus gave to the men who were to be specially His men? When Jesus saw Andrew and Peter fishing on the shores of the Sea of Galilee, He said to them, 'Follow me' (Matthew 4.19). When He saw Matthew sitting at his tax-collector's table, He said to him, 'Follow me' (Matthew 9.9). So then it is clear that to be a Christian is to follow Jesus. But what does that mean? Obviously no one can obey a command unless he knows what the command means. So what does it mean to follow Jesus?

Every word has associations. Every word is used in a certain kind of way, and when people hear a word certain pictures at once come into their minds. Now the word that the New Testament uses for *to follow*— it is *akolouthein* in Greek— had five different associations, and these associations will let us see something of what it means to be a Christian.

It is used of *a soldier following his commander*. To

follow Jesus is to look on Jesus as our commander, and to go wherever He wants us to go. It means that we never again ask, 'What is the easiest way?' We never again ask, 'Where do I want to go?' We always look to Jesus and ask, 'Where do you want me to go?' If we are to follow Jesus, we are under His orders from now on.

It is used of *a servant accompanying a master*. In the old days a man would always be followed by a slave or two; and these slaves would be ready to do on the instant whatever their master commanded them. Once we begin to follow Jesus, life has got to be like that. There is a very great missionary called Frank C. Laubach. In one of his books he writes this, 'Every college should have a good course in geography taught from the point of view of world need; then college students could find out where they were going to fit in by studying this world need.' When we are trying to find out what we should do or be, we should not be asking, 'Is this job going to further my ambitions? Is this job going to give me a scintillating career? Is this job going to bring me in more money and give me shorter hours to work?' We should be asking, 'Is this the job that Jesus wants me to do? Is this the job in which I can be most useful to Him and to my fellowmen?' If we are to follow Jesus, every day in life, and whenever any decision arises, we should be saying, 'Lord, what do you want me to do?'

It is used of *following advice given by a wiser person*. You can't avoid making decisions in life. It has been said that all life concentrates on a man at the cross-roads. We are always standing at some cross-roads or other. If we are to follow Jesus, it means that we will never take a decision without taking that decision to Him. This isn't nearly so easy as it sounds. Often when we go to people for advice, what we are really wanting is for them to say, 'Carry on: I agree with you; you're quite right.' And if they advise us to do the opposite of what we want to do, we are often quite annoyed about it. We must not only ask for Jesus advice; we must be humble enough to take it too.

It is used of *obeying the laws of the state in which a person lives*. If we live in a country, we have got to agree to abide by the laws of that country; and if we are citizens of the Kingdom of Jesus we have got to obey its laws. It would take a whole book to talk about these laws. But there are two of them which are specially important. If we follow Jesus, we must be more interested in giving than in getting. That is the most practical thing in the world. It has not only got to do with money. It has got to do with our work. If we follow Jesus, we will try to see, not how little we can do, and get away with it, but how much we can do. No real Christian ever did a bad day's work, or turned out a job that was his second best. There is an old story which tells how Jesus of Nazareth made the best ox-yokes in the whole of Galilee and that people came from all over the country to buy them, because they were so good. A follower of Jesus is even more interested in doing a good job than in the pay he gets for it. The other thing is, if we are to follow Jesus we must learn to forgive. This is not to say that we won't have differences and arguments, because it would never do if we all thought the same. But a real follower of Jesus never quarrels with anyone. A real follower of Jesus never tries to get his own back. Jesus said, 'A new commandment I give unto you, that ye love one another. By this shall all men know that ye are my disciples, if ye have love one to another' (John 13.34,35)—and that means loving the unlovable, and loving the person, who hasn't been at all nice to you. If we are followers of Jesus, we must have the same attitude to other people as Jesus had—and He forgave even the people who crucified Him.

It is used of *following a teacher's teaching and argument*. If we are to be followers of Jesus, it means that we must always be learning more and more about Him. We must always be thinking about Him and listening to Him. You don't get to know about any great subject all at once. It takes years to learn about it. It is like that with Jesus—only it takes a life-time and far more to learn all about Jesus. There should never be a day when we don't think about Him.

You could put all this very simply. When a person is a follower of Jesus, it just means that he never again does what he likes; he always does what Jesus likes. It means that never again do we say, 'What do I want to do? Where do I want to go? How do I want to work? How do I want to treat people?' It means that we must always ask, 'What does Jesus want me to do? Where does Jesus want me to go? How does Jesus want me to do this job? How does Jesus want me to treat this person?' You can see that being a follower of Jesus doesn't consist of coming to Church for an hour or two on a Sunday. It's a whole-time job. And it is the most difficult job in the world. But there are things which help us to do it, because we could never do it by ourselves, and I'll be talking to you about some of these things below.

TALKING AND LISTENING TO GOD

The great thing about the Christian life is that we don't have to live it alone and in our own strength. One of the greatest helps that we have towards living the Christian life is *prayer*.

To begin with, prayer is two things. First of all, prayer is just talking to God. Let's get certain things straight right away. Talking to God is just like talking to a friend. If you find it difficult, try putting a chair in front of you and imagining that someone is sitting there who is your dearest friend and that you are talking to him. You don't need any special kind of language for prayer. You can talk to God in the same way as you talk everyday. You don't need any special position for prayer. You can be kneeling, sitting, standing, walking, lying in bed—it's all the same. There is one thing to remember. You can't really concentrate on prayer if you are conscious of your body. That means you can't pray in an uncomfortable position. You must find a position when you forget everything except God. You don't need any special time for prayer, but it is far better to have your own fixed time. If you haven't a fixed time to pray, you will very likely find that life is so full of things that you forget to pray at all. It is good to pray first thing in the morning, even before you get up, as soon as you wake. It makes a big difference to begin the day with God, and to make God your first thought. And it is good to pray last thing at night, to take the whole day to God, to go to sleep thinking about Him.

We have said that prayer is just talking to God. That's true. But you never get the best out of a conversation when the conversation is aimless. It is better to know what you want to say when you pray. There are five kinds of prayer. There is *Invocation*. That just means asking God to be with us. Maybe it would be better to say that it is making ourselves realize that God *is* with us, for God is always with us. There is *Confession*. Confession means telling God about the wrong things we have done, and asking Him to forgive us. And, remember, the best way to show that we are sorry for having done a wrong thing is to stop doing it. If we don't, we are not really sorry at all. There is *Thanksgiving*. Thanksgiving just means thanking God for all the things we have enjoyed and all the people who have been kind to us and all the help He has given us. There is *Petition*. Petition means asking God for all the things we know that we need to live in the way He wants us to live. There is *Intercession*. Intercession means asking God to bless the people whom we love, and the people whom we know to be in trouble. You won't be able to get all the five different kinds of prayer into any one of your prayers. But you must see that as the days go on none of them is neglected.

But we said that prayer was two things. The second thing that prayer is is listening to God. You can't listen if you are always talking. We have to give God a chance to speak to us. You know that if you are with someone whom you don't know very well the great trouble is to make conversation in case there come some of these awkward pauses which are so embarrassing. But if you know someone very well indeed the two of you can sit together for a long time and say nothing at all, but be perfectly happy just because you are together. The very highest form of prayer is like that. It is just resting in silence in the presence of God.

Before very long you will come up against the problem of what people call 'unanswered prayer.' We must always remember that we will never know if any prayer is unanswered until life is at an end—and I don't think any ever is. We have always to remember certain things. God is far wiser than we are. We can't see a day or even an hour ahead. It would often happen that, if God gave us what we asked for, it would only hurt us. When you were very young you didn't get everything you wanted. If you had, it would have done you a lot more harm than good. Very often God answers our prayers in His way and not in ours, and it is sometimes only long afterwards that we see that our prayer was abundantly answered. For instance, we may pray to God for something; God does not give it to us; often it is because He has something far better in store for us, and we would have missed the fine thing if we had got what we wanted at the time. We may pray to God to take away some pain or some problem or some difficulty. Often God doesn't take it away; He does something better; He gives us strength and courage and endurance to face it and conquer it and endure it. I think that we ought to end all our prayers by saying, 'O God, I have told you what I want; but you know far better than I do what I really need; so not my will, but your will be done.'

There is just one thing more we must remember.

Prayer is never the easy way out. You could put it this way—when we pray we have to do our very best to make our own prayers come true. Think of it this way. Suppose you were sitting an examination; suppose you had done none of the work you should have done because you slacked your way through the term; suppose you got to the examination room and picked up the paper and looked at it and found that you just couldn't pass: do you think it would be any good to pray to God and say, 'O God, help me to pass this examination'? But if, on the other hand, you had done the work, but you were nervous and tense and strained, and if you prayed, 'O God, I have worked my hardest; keep me calm now; and help me to do my best,' that prayer would be answered, because you did your part. It's no good asking God to bless sick people and sad people unless you are prepared to do something to help and comfort them. It's no good asking God to bless your parents unless you are prepared to be a good son or a good daughter. Prayer isn't just pushing things off on to God. It is only when we do our best to make our prayers come true that they are fully answered.

Don't ever let a day pass without talking to God and listening to God. Don't bother about how you talk to Him, or when you talk to Him. Talk to Him just as you would to your closest friend. You'll find, if you do that, it will make all the difference in the world.

THE CHRISTIAN GUIDE-BOOK

If you are going on a journey by a road which you do not know, you will, if you are wise, consult a good map before you start out, and you will take the map with you to keep you right. If you are going to put something together, you usually get a book of instructions with it, and, if you are wise, you will follow the instructions. If you are studying some subject, there will always be some text-book prescribed, and you know that, if you are going to pass the examination at the end of the term, the text-book has to be studied. Now life is like a journey, and it is a journey along a road that is quite strange to us, because we never travel the same bit of life twice. Life is like building something up. We build a career; we build a character; we build a personality. And we who are Christians believe that life will end in an examination and a scrutiny before God. And we are fortunate in this—we do possess a book which is a map for the road, a book which gives us instructions how to build, a book which is the text-book of the Christian life. That book is the Bible. And now that you have started on the Christian way you must read your Bible.

When you start to read the Bible there are certain things which you must bear in mind.

One is that it took a long time to write the Bible. The earliest books in the Old Testament were written away back somewhere around 900 B.C., and the latest books in the New Testament were written somewhere after A.D. 100. It took more than 1,000 years to write the Bible. Now a nation grows up a lot in more than 1,000 years. In British history 1,000 years would take us back to about the time of Alfred the Great. At that time there was no such thing as gas or electric light or a motor car; there was no such thing as sanitation and health services; there was no such thing as a newspaper or a printed book; there was no such thing in Britain as sugar or a potato or tobacco. People still thought that the earth was flat and that the sun went round the earth. Life was very different. There has been a great growth and a great development in life in 1,000 years. Now the Bible is like that. It tells and shows us how people learned more and more about God. It wasn't that God changed; it was that men's knowledge of God changed. When you start algebra, you don't start with the binomial theorem; you work up to it bit by bit. It was that way with men's knowledge of God. When you come to bits of the Old Testament which are savage and bloodthirsty don't get worried about them. When you come to bits when the Israelites think it is a fine thing to wipe out the men and women and children of some city, don't be puzzled. That is all the length they had got by that time. They were still learning but they had still a lot to learn. When you read things in the older parts of the Bible which don't seem Christian, don't worry about them. These are stages on the way, steps in the development by which people slowly came to know about God.

Another thing you will find is that the Bible can be a very difficult book. It is made more difficult by the fact that our Authorised Version was translated into English in A.D. 1611. Language changes a lot in more than 300 years. For that reason you would be better with a new translation. You could get Moffatt's translation, or The American Revised Standard Version. These contain the whole Bible. You could get E. V. Rieu's translation of the Four Gospels, which is one of the Penguin Classics. You could get J. B. Phillips' *Letters to Young Churches*, which is a splendid modern translation of the letters in the New Testament. You will find the Bible a lot easier to understand in one of these translations. Even then the Bible can be difficult. But you must remember this—we must not only read the Bible; we must *study* the Bible. It is a grand thing to study the Bible with some of the Daily Bible Readings which are available, and it is better yet to study it in a Bible Study discussion group. If you come on parts of the Bible that you still can't understand, your minister will be delighted to talk them over with you, and to try to explain them to you. And there is one thing always to remember—even if there are bits of the Bible which you cannot understand, there is plenty left which you *can* understand. Spurgeon, the great preacher, was once talking about this. He said, 'Suppose I am eating a very nice piece of fish; and suppose I come on a bone; what do I do? I don't fling the whole piece of fish away. I just put the bone at the side of the plate and leave it there and go on with the rest of the fish.' If there are bits of the Bible which are really too difficult, it is best just to leave them aside—some day they will become clear—and to go on with the bits you can understand.

Perhaps you feel that the Bible is a very big book—after all, the Bible isn't only one book, it is 66 books all bound together—and you wonder where to start. The Bible exists to tell us one thing—to tell us about Jesus. So, then, start with the gospels which Mark and Luke wrote. These give us the picture of Jesus. Then go on and read *Acts*, and see the birth and growth of the Christian Church. But all this could never have happened without a long preparation. So go back now and read the history books of the Old Testament, and read the prophets with their dreams of God's Great One who was to come. Read the Psalms to see how people sang and prayed to God in the old days. And then read the New Testament letters to see all the problems which faced the Church as it grew up.

When you do this remember two things. First, sometimes read a great big part of the Bible. Read the whole of Mark's gospel at a sitting. That's the only way to get the sweep of the story. When you read a novel you don't read twenty or thirty lines at a time. You read the whole story. If you read *Mark* or *Acts* through at one or two sittings, you will be swept on by the story as it unfolds before you. Second, be regular in your reading. Read a portion of the Bible every day in life. It is a good thing to read it last thing at night before you go to sleep.

This book, the Bible, is God's word as no other book is, because it is written by men to whom God could speak because they lived closer to Him than anyone else. It is our map, our instruction, our textbook. You may begin reading it as a duty; you will end reading it as one of the greatest pleasures in life.

May you find joy in reading and in studying the word of God.

THE CHURCH AND YOU

By this time you are either a member of the Church or you are thinking of becoming one. Now, if you are a member of any society, you want to know just what that society stands for, what it offers, and what it is out to do. You must be feeling that way about the Church.

The Church is a fellowship of people who have all accepted Jesus as their Saviour, their Master and their Lord. The first creed the Church ever had was very simple. It was quite simply 'Jesus Christ is Lord.' Paul knew that it was the great hope of God that a day would come when every tongue would confess that 'Jesus Christ is Lord' (Philippians 2.11). If you say, 'Jesus Christ is Lord,'' what do you mean? To put it at its simplest, you mean that for you Jesus is unique, that for you there is nobody like Him on earth or in heaven, and that you are prepared to give to Him a love, a loyalty and an obedience that you are not prepared to give to anyone else in all the world.

Now, once you see that, another thing becomes clear. If the Church is the fellowship of all those who say, 'Jesus Christ is Lord,' it means that your congregation is not the Church, not even your denomination is the Church; the Church is far bigger and far wider than that. The Church is composed of all those who in every age, and every land, and every Church have said and are saying, 'Jesus Christ is Lord.' When you enter into the Church, you enter into a tremendous thing, a thing as wide as the world, and as vast as eternity, a thing which includes every nation under the sun, a thing which embraces those who live and those who have died in the faith. If you are a member of the Church, you are a member of the greatest society on earth.

In Christ there is no East or West,
In Him no South or North,
But one great fellowship of love
Throughout the whole wide earth.

But the Church does not exist solely to give us something; we exist to give the Church something. What is the Church designed to do? Paul used a great phrase to describe the Church; he called it *the body of Christ* (I Corinthians 12.27). What did he mean by that? Think of it this way. Jesus is no longer here in this world in the body. His Spirit is here; His presence is here; but He is not here in the body. So, then, if Jesus wants something done, He has to get someone to do it for Him. If He wants a child taught, He has to get someone to teach him. If He wants a sick person helped, He has to get a doctor to help him. If He wants a book written, or a message brought to men, or a job done, He has to get someone to do it. We have to be the body of Christ, hands to work for Him, a mouth to speak for Him, feet to run upon His errands. Quite literally, we in the Church have to be the body through which Jesus works.

He has no hands but our hands
To do His work today;
He has no feet but our feet
To lead men in His way;
He has no voice but our voice
To tell men how He died;
He has no help but our help
To bring them to His side.

We have to be Jesus' body, hands and feet for Him to use; we have to carry on His work. What, then, was His work, that work which we must carry on? Jesus came doing three things.

First, Jesus came *preaching*. The word that is used for preaching in the New Testament literally means *a herald's announcement*. Preaching is the proclamation of certainties. Now it isn't only the minister who has got to be certain about things. *You* have to be certain. That means that you have to think things out and think them through for yourself. You must never just accept anything because someone else says it. You have got to think it out for yourself. And remember this— the Bible does not say, 'I know *what* I have believed.' It says, 'I know *whom* I have believed.' A Christian, a member of the Church, is someone who knows Jesus personally, and who is sure of Him.

Second, Jesus came *teaching*. Teaching means telling and showing others the truth of the Christian faith. Here is the difficult thing. We really prove our Christianity, not by our words, but by our lives. If we, as Church members, have to show people what Christianity is, we do not do it by talking about it, but by doing it. It has been said that 'a saint is someone in whom Christ lives again.' We have to show men what Christ is like. And we have to show them that not just in the Church. It is easy in the Church where everything is reverent and quiet and peaceful. We have to show what Christ is like in the shop, the factory, the office, the playing-field, the street, the home, the school, the college, wherever we work. As Church members our tremendous task is to show others what Jesus is like.

Third, Jesus came *healing*. That is to say, Jesus did not stop with words: He turned His words into deeds of love and help and kindness. Someone has said, 'An ideal is not yours until it comes out of your finger-tips.' As Church members we have to turn our Christian belief and ideals into acts of service and of love towards all in need. It is not a case of talking about the Christian life; it is a case of *living* the Christian life.

Frank Laubach, the great missionary, worked out a simple formula for the Christian life. 'The soul will have one hand reaching to the sky asking, "Father, how can I help you help the world?" and will listen for His reply. The other hand will reach down and out to humanity all around the world, asking, "Everybody, everywhere, how can I help you?" Wide open *upward* all the time, and wide-open *outward* all the time.'

The Church is the body of Christ. What a glorious privilege it is to be the hands and feet and voice of Christ! And that's your privilege when you enter into that membership which is always open to you.

God make you a good member of His Church.

YOU AND THE CHURCH

When we are thinking of membership of the Church and of what it must mean to us, there are certain questions which we at once wish to ask.

We are bound to ask, first of all, *Why* go to Church? What is the idea in going to Church? I would like you to think of, and always to remember, three reasons for going to Church.

First, *to go to Church is an opportunity to demonstrate where our loyalty lies.* If every Saturday afternoon people see you going down the road and into a certain football ground, they haven't much doubt where your loyalty lies; they soon know what team you support. And if they see you go down the road every Sunday to the Church, they know what side you are on. To go to Church is to show that we are on Jesus' side.

Second, *to go to Church is to get help to live in the right way.* Sometimes we get queer pictures of things in our minds. A small boy once said that he saw the days of the week as the carriages in a train, and Sunday as the engine which pulled the train. When we go to Church we get guidance to settle our problems, strength to face our temptations, the reminder of what is right and true and good, the assurance that Jesus is always with us. In the Church we get the standard and the ideal of the Christian life held up to us, and we get help to live up to that standard.

Third, *to go to Church is to go to worship God.* This is the most important thing of all. It is very hard to define in words what worship is. A friend once went to visit a famous minister. In the evening, when it was very dark, the minister suggested that they should go for a walk on the hillside behind the house. They went. When they were just about to come home, the minister said, 'I think out here we ought to pray.' So he prayed, and the friend said afterwards, 'I was almost afraid to stretch out my hand in the dark in case I should touch God.' That is what worship is. Worship is that which brings us close to God, that which makes us feel aware of God. You could put it quite simply—we come to Church to meet God.

Then, I think we must ask another question, *How*

should I go to Church? Now here is a thing that we *must* remember. We do not go to Church only to *get* something; we go to *give* something. We ought to come to Church *prepared* in mind and in heart. It is not enough to start at the last minute and rush down the road. Even if it is only for a moment or two, we should prepare ourselves before we come. We should think what we are going to do; and we should, just in a sentence or two, pray to God to help us really to share in the service. The Jews had a lovely saying, 'They pray best together who have first prayed alone.' You see, the atmosphere of a service makes all the difference. I don't know if you have ever realized it, but it is the congregation which preaches half the sermon, and helps to make the prayers real. If there is a real atmosphere of expectancy and of eagerness to listen, it makes all the difference in the world. We can help to produce that atmosphere if we prepare ourselves before we come.

Then, again, I think that we are bound to ask, *How often* should I come to Church? There is only one real answer to that question, and it is, 'Every Sunday, if I possibly can.' There is a great deal to be said for habits—so long as they are good habits; and we ought to get to the stage when we feel there is something wrong with the week if we haven't been to Church. There are a great many people who say that this is God's world and that you can meet with and worship God anywhere. That's quite true. But think of it this way. Suppose you were listening to a great orchestra playing great music, would you enjoy it better if you were all alone in a vast empty hall, or if the hall was crowded with people? Suppose you were watching some great sports event, would you enjoy it better if you were the sole spectator, or if you were one of a great crowd? It is one of the facts of life that we get a far bigger thrill out of a thing when we are one of a crowd; it is far more exciting; the atmosphere is far more electric. We are built for what someone called 'togetherness.' I don't for a minute say that you can't worship God by the seashore, and on the hillside, and on the open road; but I do say that it is when we worship together that we feel God closest of all. And, after all, we have a great example here. Jesus went into the Synagogue at Nazareth on the Sabbath day *as His custom was* (Luke 4.16). If it was His habit to go to the Church of His people, surely it should be ours too.

There is one other thing about you and the Church that must be spoken of. If you become a member of the Church, you will have to face the responsibility of supporting the Church with your money. I don't see why we should feel awkward speaking about this. The Church has to pay its way like any other organisation, and we are the Church. But there is far more to it than that. We would like to help the people who are less fortunate than we are; we can't do it always personally ourselves; but the Church has its social service and our money can go where we can't go. We would like to tell people who had never heard of Him about Jesus. We can't all be foreign missionaries and go abroad. But where we cannot go our money can go. When we think what we are giving for, and who we are giving to, it should be a thrill and not an unpleasant duty to support the Church.

Someone tells of a person who was doing a crossword puzzle. They had come to a word of six letters. The first two letters were 'CH' and the last two were 'CH'. What could the word be? This person then got the third last letter from a clue that ran in the opposite direction. It was 'R'. Now the word ran 'CH-RCH'. At once the person saw it. 'I've discovered it,' he said, 'It takes "U", to make it Church.' It takes *you* to make the Church. You can't get on without the Church, and the Church can't get on without you. I hope and pray that in the days to come your life will be richer for the Church, and the life of the Church will be richer for you.

THE SACRED SERVICE OF THE CHURCH

When you become a full member of the Church, there is one special difference which it makes to you. You are allowed to come to what we sometimes call *The Communion Service*, and sometimes *The Sacrament of the Lord's Supper*. Obviously, that is a very special service; and it is most important that we should know and understand something of what we are doing when we come to it. The fact that Jesus said of this service, 'This do in remembrance of me' (I Corinthians 11.24) gives to it a place that is all its own.

There are four things, which, if we remember them and think of them, will help us to come to this service as we ought to come.

First, the Communion Service puts the love of Jesus in a picture and in a dramatic action for us. The old Hebrew prophets used to have an interesting way of doing things. When they could not persuade people to listen to their words, they used to do something which

123

put their message into a picture, and which people could not help seeing. For instance, when Jeremiah was sure that disaster was coming to the people, and when they would not listen to him, he made a yoke and went about wearing it round his neck, to show the people what was going to happen to them (Jeremiah 27.1-8). Our Communion Service is like that. When the bread is broken, Jesus is saying to us, 'Look! That is how my body was broken for you.' When the wine is poured out, Jesus is saying to us, 'Look! That is how my blood was shed for you.' Abraham Lincoln gave the slaves in America their freedom. In the end he was assassinated. When his funeral was passing through the streets, an old Negro woman stood watching with a little black boy at her side. As the coffin passed, she said to the boy through her tears, 'Take a good look at him. He died for you.' That is exactly what the Communion Service is saying to us about Jesus.

Second, the Communion Service takes ordinary things to speak to us of eternal things. This is the kind of thing that can happen quite often in ordinary everyday life. Often we keep a thing, which is of no value in itself, because when we touch it and handle it and look at it, it brings back memories of someone or something. The thing is an ordinary thing, but it speaks to us of things and people far beyond itself. Someone describes a scene at Nelson's funeral. He was buried in St. Paul's and his coffin was carried in by a detachment of sailors of the Royal Navy. They laid the body of the greatest of all the Admirals to rest. 'With reverence and with efficiency they lowered the body of the world's greatest Admiral into its tomb; then, as though answering a sharp order from the quarter-deck, they all seized the Union Jack with which the coffin was covered and tore it into separate pieces.' Then each man took his own piece as a souvenir of the illustrious dead. It was only a little bit of coloured cloth they had kept, but in it there was something of Nelson himself. The Sacrament is like that. The things we touch and handle and taste are only common bread and wine, but they speak to us and remind us of something far beyond themselves; they speak to us of the love of Jesus who suffered and died for us.

Third, when we sit at the Communion Table we take an oath of loyalty to Jesus Christ. The word *sacrament* comes from the Latin word *sacramentum*. The sacramentum was the oath of loyalty which every Roman soldier took to the Emperor when he joined the Roman army. So then to go forward to the Communion Table is to take an oath of loyalty to Jesus. That is very important. From the time we sit at that table, we are pledged to Jesus. Other people know that we have done it; people outside the Church know that we have done it. The result is that the honour of the Church and the honour of Jesus are in our hands. People judge the Church by our life and conduct. Dick Sheppard, who used to talk often with people outside the Church, and even hostile to the Church, and who used to try to meet their arguments and objections said that, in his experience, the greatest handicap the Church has is the unsatisfactory lives of professing Christians. That is very true. When we come to the Communion Table, we are saying what Peter once said to Jesus, 'Though I should die with Thee, yet will I not deny Thee' (Matthew 26.35). We have to see to it that, with the help which Jesus can give us, we never break our pledge.

Fourth, the sacrament is more than any of these things. It is the way in which we come into direct contact with Jesus. It is the experience of life that certain places bring us into contact with certain people even when they are not there. In such places we feel very near to those of whom we are thinking, even if they are miles away, and even if they are no longer in the world. At the Communion Table we have that chance to feel Jesus near us and to make real and living contact with Him. That doesn't happen automatically. Before it can happen we must come with love and expectation in our hearts and minds. And if we do we shall certainly meet Jesus there.

If you are coming to the Communion Service for the first time, I hope that it will be a day you will never forget. If you have been before, I hope that you will meet Jesus more really than ever before. And all through your life, I hope and pray that every time you come to the Communion Table, you will really see Jesus.